'To live through Josephine – that is the story of my life.' This was written by one of the greatest men in history soon after his wedding with the alluring, worldly Josephine de Beauharnais. Throughout their stormy and passionate marriage – and even after their painful divorce – they never really ceased to love each other. Without him, she led a solitary, unremarkable life; he died with her name on his lips. Their poignant love story is one of the most famous in the world.

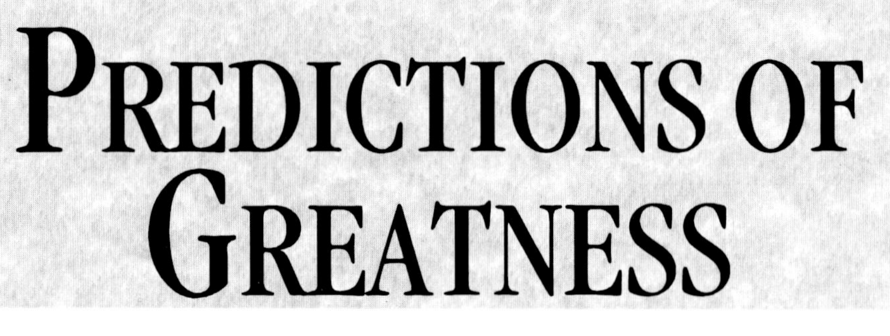

PREDICTIONS OF GREATNESS

Jean-Loup Charmet

WHILE NAPOLEON'S FUTURE MILITARY SUCCESSES WERE FORESHADOWED IN A SNOWBALL FIGHT HE ORCHESTRATED AS A BOY, THE YOUNG JOSEPHINE'S RISE TO POWER WAS PREDICTED BY A MULATTO WOMAN IN MARTINIQUE

A youthful portrait of Napoleon's mother, Letizia* above. *She was a dominant figure in Napoleon's life and, Napoleon claimed, was largely responsible for his greatness

The large, shuttered stone house in Ajaccio, Corsica,* below, *where Napoleon was born. Although not rich, his family was well-connected and comfortably off by Corsican standards

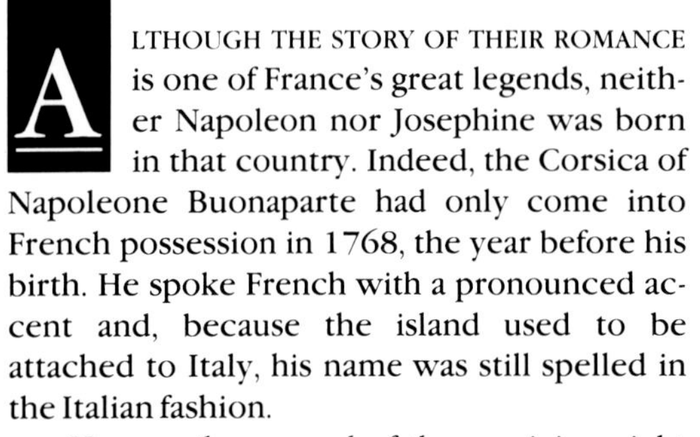

ALTHOUGH THE STORY OF THEIR ROMANCE is one of France's great legends, neither Napoleon nor Josephine was born in that country. Indeed, the Corsica of Napoleone Buonaparte had only come into French possession in 1768, the year before his birth. He spoke French with a pronounced accent and, because the island used to be attached to Italy, his name was still spelled in the Italian fashion.

He was the second of the surviving eight children born to Carlo and Letizia Buonaparte. His unusual first name, that of a Greek saint, was a tribute to his great uncle. Carlo was a lawyer from the minor nobility who had married a beautiful, semi-literate wife. Letizia, though utterly devoted to her brood of children, was an uncompromisingly tough matriarch.

Napoleon was considered a difficult child by his mother, who gave him the largest share of her attention. Although she spoiled him as a very young child, she was later severe in correcting any misbehaviour in an attempt to mould his character. Napoleon would later credit her with being an important influence on his adult life and its successes.

Fontenay: Napoleon's Birthplace, Malmaison/© Photo RMN

The Lion of the Valley

Napoleon's Corsican childhood ended at the age of nine, when he was sent to be educated in France for a career as an army officer.

At his military school in Brienne, he was mercilessly taunted on account of his Corsican accent and his awkwardness. Although lonely and often seriously depressed, he was a brilliant student and he worked hard. Napoleon excelled in history, geography and especially maths. To Napoleon, the mastery of maths meant power.

The conditions at Brienne, where Napoleon spent five years, were tough. Each boy occupied his own small, sparse 'cell'. Furnishings included only a camp bed with a single blanket and a jug and basin for cold water washes. The days were strictly controlled from 6am to 10pm and, at night, the boys were locked into their individual rooms.

There were, however, brief moments of respite, one of which occurred during the winter of 1783-84. After a long period of heavy snowfalls and confinement indoors, the boys were bored and restless. The young Napoleon suggested that they build snow fortresses, divide themselves into two factions and fight a battle with snowballs. The snowball fight lasted for two weeks until the boys began to mix stones

♔ ***The earliest known sketch from life of the young Napoleon* left, *made in 1785 while he was a cadet in Paris. After graduating as a sub-lieutenant, he was sent to learn the profession of soldier in provincial garrisons. A large part of the pittance he earned was sent to his widowed mother in Corsica***

Mary Evans Picture Library

♔ ***The first signs of leadership: Napoleon directing the snowball fight at Brienne* above. *In this mock battle, which lasted two weeks, Napoleon supervised the construction of the fortresses, which conformed to standard military architecture, and appointed himself commander***

with snow and the game turned into a real war with a number of injuries.

When Napoleon was 15, he won a scholarship to an advanced military school in Paris, from which he graduated as a sub-lieutenant in 1785. There followed two miserable and poverty-stricken years doing garrison duty in various provincial towns.

But with the outbreak of the French Revolution in 1789 Napoleon proved himself worthy of his unusual first name, which means 'lion of the valley'. It was he rather than his eldest brother, Joseph, who took chief responsibility for Letizia, now widowed, and his younger brothers and sisters during the turbulent revolutionary years. He established them in Marseilles on the mainland.

Despite his military education and his Corsican background, Napoleon never wavered in his loyalty to the new republic of France. The new society offered unparalleled opportunities for advancement. In 1793 the 24-year-old soldier dislodged an invading Spanish-British fleet from Toulon harbour. He was promoted to brigadier-general.

Burning to set up house

In 1794, when his elder brother Joseph married Julie Clary, the daughter of a Marseilles merchant, Napoleon expressed an interest in her dark-eyed sister Desirée. While the negotiations between the two families proceeded he could not disguise his impatience, writing home from Paris: 'I am burning to set up house ... either an arrangement must be made (with Desirée) or the whole thing must be broken off.' But, alas, Desirée's mother decided that 'One Bonaparte in the family is enough.' It had been only natural for Napoleon to look south when he thought of marriage because he felt out of place in Paris society, and sophisticated French women intimidated him.

The year which saw Napoleon rejected by Desirée Clary's family also saw him temporarily in hot water with France's political authority, the Convention. He was imprisoned because his meteoric promotion had happened under Robespierre, the virtual dictator of France during the Reign of Terror. But he stayed cool and,

NAPOLEON'S FIRST LOVE

Napoleon's first love was Desirée Clary, the 16-year-old sister of his brother's wife. Dark-haired, small and slight, she was intensely feminine and sweet-natured, Napoleon fell in love with her and though their marriage was forbidden, he bombarded her with love letters. Within a year, his passion, conducted from Paris, had worn off and he broke off the affair with surprising tact and kindness. Desirée subsequently married one of Napoleon's marshals, Bernodotte, and became Queen of Sweden. Her descendants still sit on the Swedish throne

Gerard: Desirée Clary (detail), Versailles/© Photo RMN

♔ ***In Paris* above, *Napoleon felt awkward, provincial and unsophisticated beside his fellow officers who were often rich, with dandified clothes and aristocratic airs. Alone, he often frequented cheap restaurants, studying papers on military strategy as he ate a meagre supper***

since his military talent was never in doubt, he emerged after a matter of days, to further promotion, and work in Paris.

The nonchalant Creole

Like Napoleon, Josephine started life with a different first name. She was born Marie-Josèphe-Rose Tascher de la Pagerie, in 1763, and was known as 'Rose' for more than half of her life. She was the first of three daughters born to an aristocratic French couple who had settled in the sugar and rum colony of Martinique. Society there was gracious and well-mannered. Josephine grew up on the family estate, a sugar plantation in Trois Ilets. Althoûgh short of money, the Taschers were well connected and, thanks to plentiful slave labour, the lifestyle was relaxed and self indulgent. Indeed, the very word 'Creole', which then meant people of Spanish or French blood brought up in the Caribbean colonies, was synonymous with a sensuous laziness.

Josephine inherited this 'Creole nonchalance' and when she became Empress of the French people marvelled at the way in which she could be idle without being bored. Whereas her consort Napoleon's harsh Corsican accent jarred on Parisian ears, Josephine's Creole drawl was considered seductive. All her life Josephine adored exotic flowers – jasmine, orchids and bougainvillea – and the flamboyant plumage of tropical birds. These were the sights and smells of her youth. As a party piece in Paris she would sometimes wrap a brightly coloured scarf around her head and dance, just as the sugarworkers of Martinique had done.

Even the most malicious of Josephine's detractors affirmed how genuinely charming she

'exceptionally sweet disposition'

JOSEPHINE'S FATHER ON JOSEPHINE

was. The family servants and slaves in Martinique remembered her with special affection and when Josephine settled in France she regularly sent home for maids and nurses for her own household. After all, it had been a mulatto nurse who had held her as a three-year-old and brought her to safety in 1766 when a hurricane devastated Martinique. It was also a mulatto woman who prophesied that Rose would marry young, be unhappy, be widowed and then be 'more than Queen of France'.

When Josephine was nine, her parents sent

© Collection Viollet

♔ ***Alexandre de Beauharnais* right, *seemed the epitome of the handsome, young French aristocrat of pre-Revolutionary days. In fact, he was a 'drawing-room liberal' with advanced political ideas. When the Revolution broke out, he joined the reformers and rose to eminence as the person who organized the arrest of the royal family. His fall from power, and his execution by guillotine, was as swift as his rise***

her to Fort Royal, on the opposite side of the bay from Trois Ilets, to be educated. There she studied for five years with the nuns at the Convent of the Ladies of Providence.

Mademoiselle Tascher de la Pagerie was leaving her convent school, having completed an exceptionally superficial education, when the boy who would fulfil her prophecy was entering military school. It was now time to think about marriage and her Aunt Edmée, who lived in France, obliged by coming up with the ideal candidate in the shape of her godson, Alexandre de Beauharnais. Upon marriage, he stood to inherit a fortune as well as the title of Vicomte.

La Vicomtesse de Beauharnais

With such material considerations at the forefronts of their minds, the matchmakers were not very romantic. Her father provided a matter-of-fact description of his eldest daughter's 'exceptionally sweet disposition', of her 'fine complexion and beautiful eyes and arms' and of her talents as a singer. From France the reply came, 'Bring us whichever of your daughters you consider most likely to suit my son.' The marriage papers were forwarded to Martinique with the name of the groom filled in and the space for the bride's name left blank.

Josephine's first experience of love was doomed to be a cruel, trying one. She was 16 when she arrived in a cold French port to meet the 19-year-old Alexandre de Beauharnais. She spent less than 15 months in the company of this husband, who made no secret of his impatience with her. She was a shy, backward little Creole, and, by the standards of French high society, completely uneducated. Under Alexandre's strict instructions Josephine immediately embarked on a complete course of improvement, her husband correcting the style of her letters to him and making harsh comments on her progress.

She hoped that the birth of two children, Eugène in 1781 and Hortense in 1783, would make him love her more. But Alexandre could never warm to his imported bride because he was madly in love with his mistress, whom he had met before Josephine had even arrived in

♔ ***This delightful, early portrait of Josephine*** below ***was painted by her good friend, Jean-Baptiste Isabey. It is thought that this wispy, ethereal picture is the one that Napoleon refers to in a love letter at the very beginning of their relationship, when he wrote to her, overwhelmed with love, 'I awaken full of you. Between your portrait and the memory of our intoxicating night, my senses have had no respite . . .'***

♔ ***Far from France on the tropical island of Martinique, the fortune-teller's predictions about Josephine's future*** below ***must have seemed wildly remote. But like many idle and pleasure-loving young women, Josephine could fantasize about her future life. Her hopes were pinned on going to Paris, the city of her dreams, a hope fulfilled in 1779.***

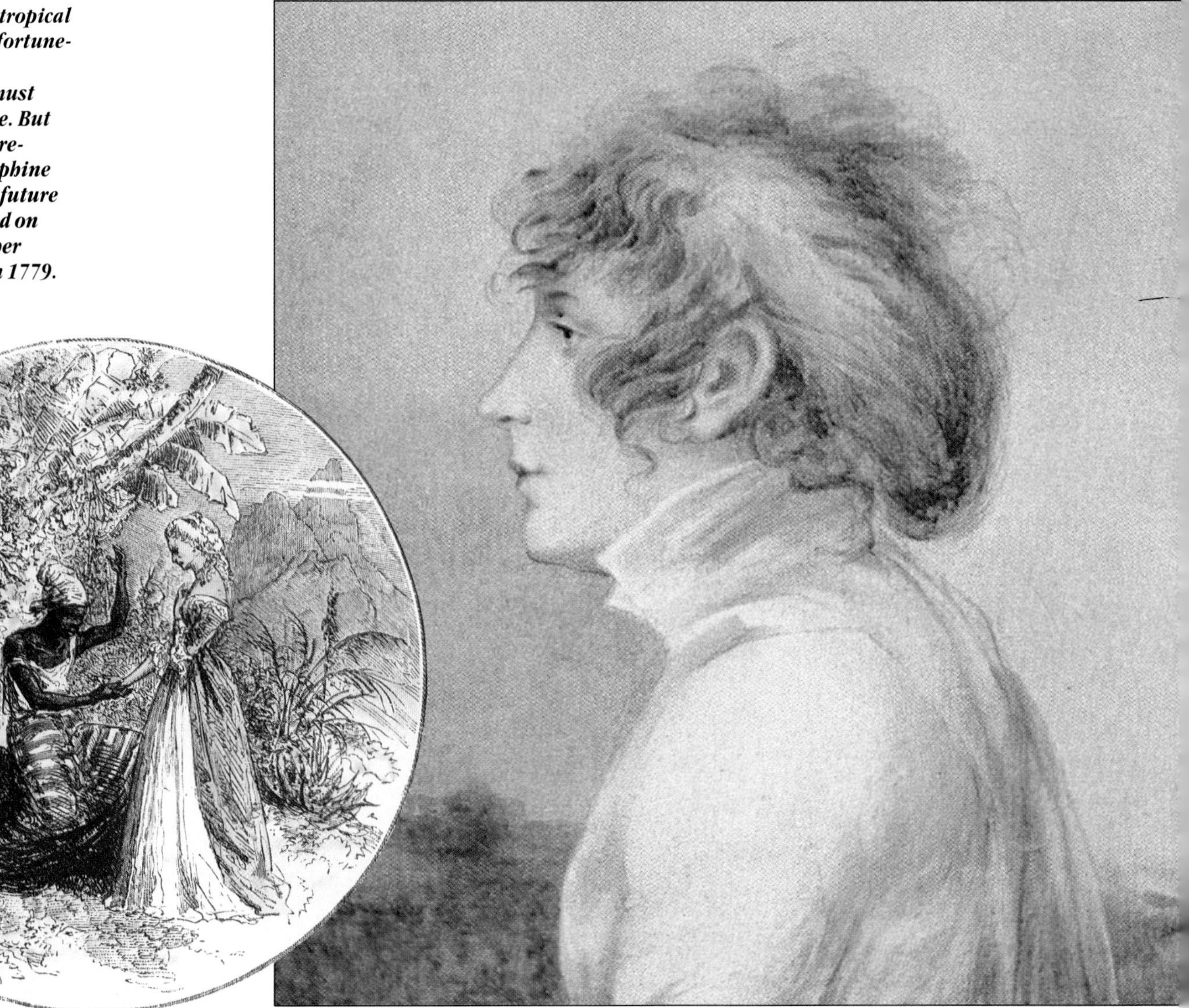

Jean-Loup Charmet

♕ ***Josephine became the mistress of Paul Barras*** above ***in 1795. Although condemned by many of his contemporaries as 'shameless and debauched', he gave Josephine a certain security and luxury and he introduced her to the pleasures of Paris society***

♕ ***While in prison and facing execution, Josephine sought love and reassurance in the arms of the dashing, young, 26-year-old General Lazare Hoche*** left

France. Things became so disagreeable that a formal separation was necessary.

Ladies in the Vicomtesse de Beauharnais' position generally retired to a convent. This was not as onerous as it sounds, for the convent of Pentemont was a large, comfortably furnished mansion resorted to by ladies of high society when they had domestic troubles. For Josephine it served as a sort of finishing school where she was able to observe, and learn, the manners and style of the aristocracy. Then the French Revolution intervened.

The impact of the revolution

In keeping with his advanced ideas Alexandre was a fervent revolutionary, even a signatory to the death warrant of the King. But as the revolution intensified, and the Terror began, men like Alexandre de Beauharnais became its victims. When he was imprisoned, so was his wife, and when he was guillotined in August 1794, she expected the same fate.

But her months in prison were also a time for romance, for it was there that she met and fell in love with General Hoche. The brief but ardent affair, which lasted only 20 days, took place in the darkness of Hoche's cell.

On 24 July 1794 Alexandre Beauharnais was sent to the scaffold. Josephine should have

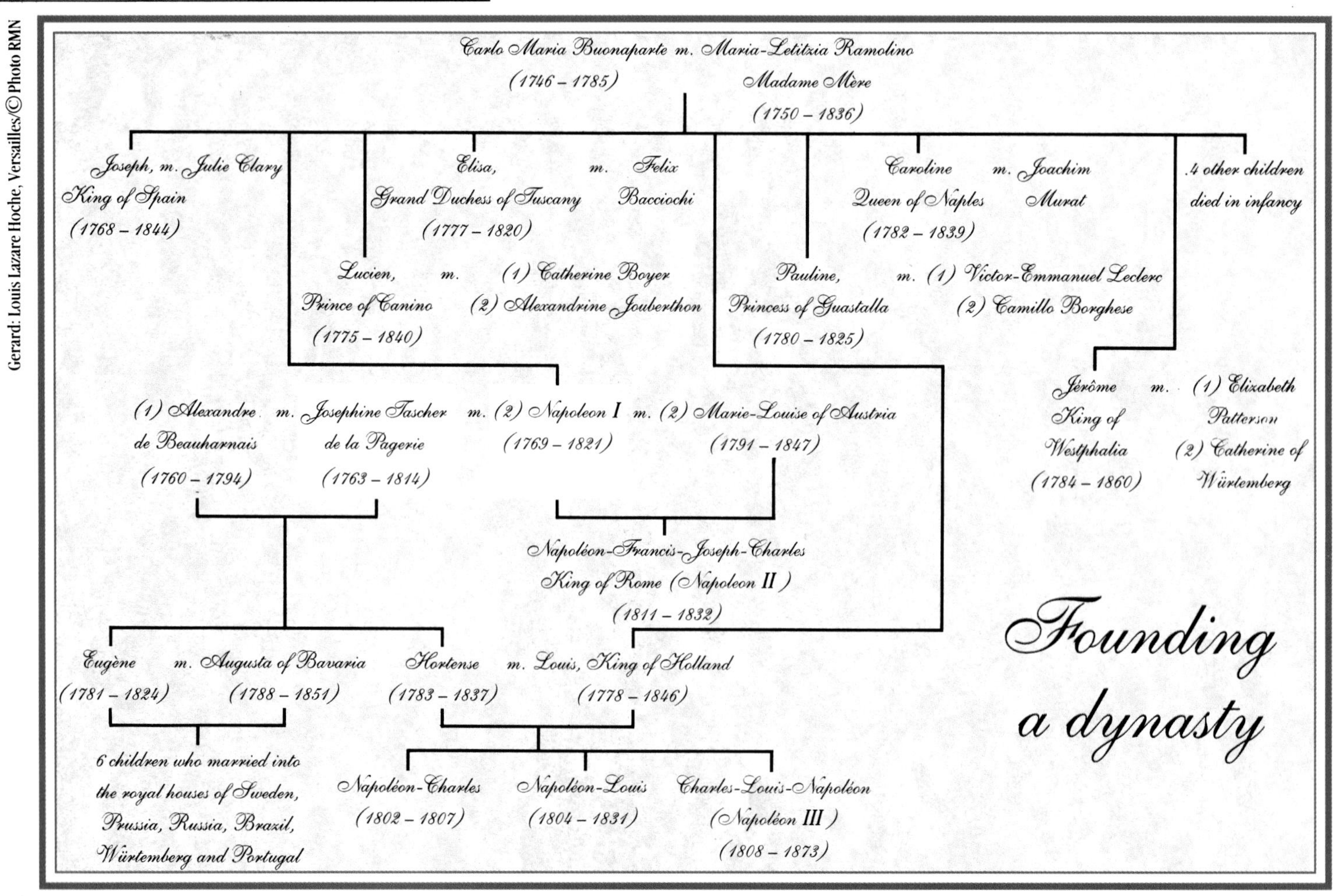

followed her husband but, by an exceptional stroke of luck, her life was spared. Her dossier had disappeared thanks to an employee of the Commission of Public Safety (the body responsible for the Terror). This man, Delperch de la Bussière, regularly removed the documents of those he wanted by eating them.

Josephine's faith in the fortune predicted for her was vindicated when, just three days after Alexandre's execution, Robespierre himself was killed. With his death the Terror ended. The Vicomtesse de Beauharnais was now a widowed mother of two but she was not as vulnerable as the 16-year-old bride of Alexandre de Beauharnais had been. The Creole duckling had become a swan who knew how to survive. She had learned how to charm the powerful men who would ensure her survival and the success of her children. Accordingly, it was not long before she found a sponsor in Paul Barras. He was a powerful and corrupt politician, the leading figure in the post-revolutionary government and young General Bonaparte's boss. Barras had amassed a great fortune during the revolution and lived like a king, surrounded by the most elegant women in Paris.

'Naturally and invariably gracious.'

A PARISIAN FRIEND ON JOSEPHINE

It was as a prisoner during the revolution that Josephine had first become friendly with Paul Barras's most famous, and most beautiful, other protégée, Thérèse Tallien. She had called upon the Beauharnais children, Eugène and Hortense, to assure them that their mother would be released. Although her many lovers and illegitimate children meant that she never qualified for a position in the imperial court, Thérèse Tallien remained a close friend of Josephine'. It was Madame Tallien, Madame Beauharnais and Madame Récamier, one of Paris's most beautiful and witty hostesses, who started the fashion for white, filmy dresses in the style of ancient Greek goddesses.

There are various descriptions of Josephine at this time. One friend noted that she was 'naturally and invariably gracious' and went on to comment, 'There is also a certain intriguing air of langourousness about her – a Creole characteristic.' Her charms – the gracefulness of her movements, the sparkle in her eyes, the low, musical voice – were rated in terms of their special femininity. In other, modern, words, Josephine was very sexy.

Madame Tallien, Bibliothèque Nationale, Paris/Lauros/Giraudon

Therese Tallien above *introduced Josephine to Paul Barras and other high-ranking government officials. She was typical of the kind of worldly-wise, beautiful and amoral women who were society hostesses in Paris at this time*

THE REIGN OF TERROR

The reign of terror lasted from 1793 to 1794 when Robespierre effectively dominated the whole government and fanatically set about suppressing any form of opposition to his word or any call for moderation against the hundreds of daily executions which took place throughout the country. No one who had played any role in the Revolution was safe; nor was anyone connected with the aristocracy. The terror came to an end when Robespierre fell victim to his own excesses and was arrested and guillotined in July 1794

Moullard: Robespierre & St Just leave for the Guillotine, Galerie Dijol Paris/Bridgeman/Giraudon

A New Dynasty

Although hereditary monarchy had been banished 'forever' just 12 years before, Napoleon insisted on all the trappings of royalty, including orb, sceptre and crown, for his Coronation as Emperor in 1804. As founder of a new royal house which he believed would dominate Europe, Napoleon chose his regalia to reflect the style of such previous European conquerors as Charlemagne and the Roman Emperors

♔ Bonaparte's wish was that he should carry the same ornaments of office at his Coronation as Charlemagne had at his investiture in 800 A.D. However, none had survived that could be established as authentic, and the crown he used *below* was a reproduction. Made of gilded silver, and set with cameos and precious stones, it was carried into the ceremony on a velvet cushion by one of Napoleon's marshals

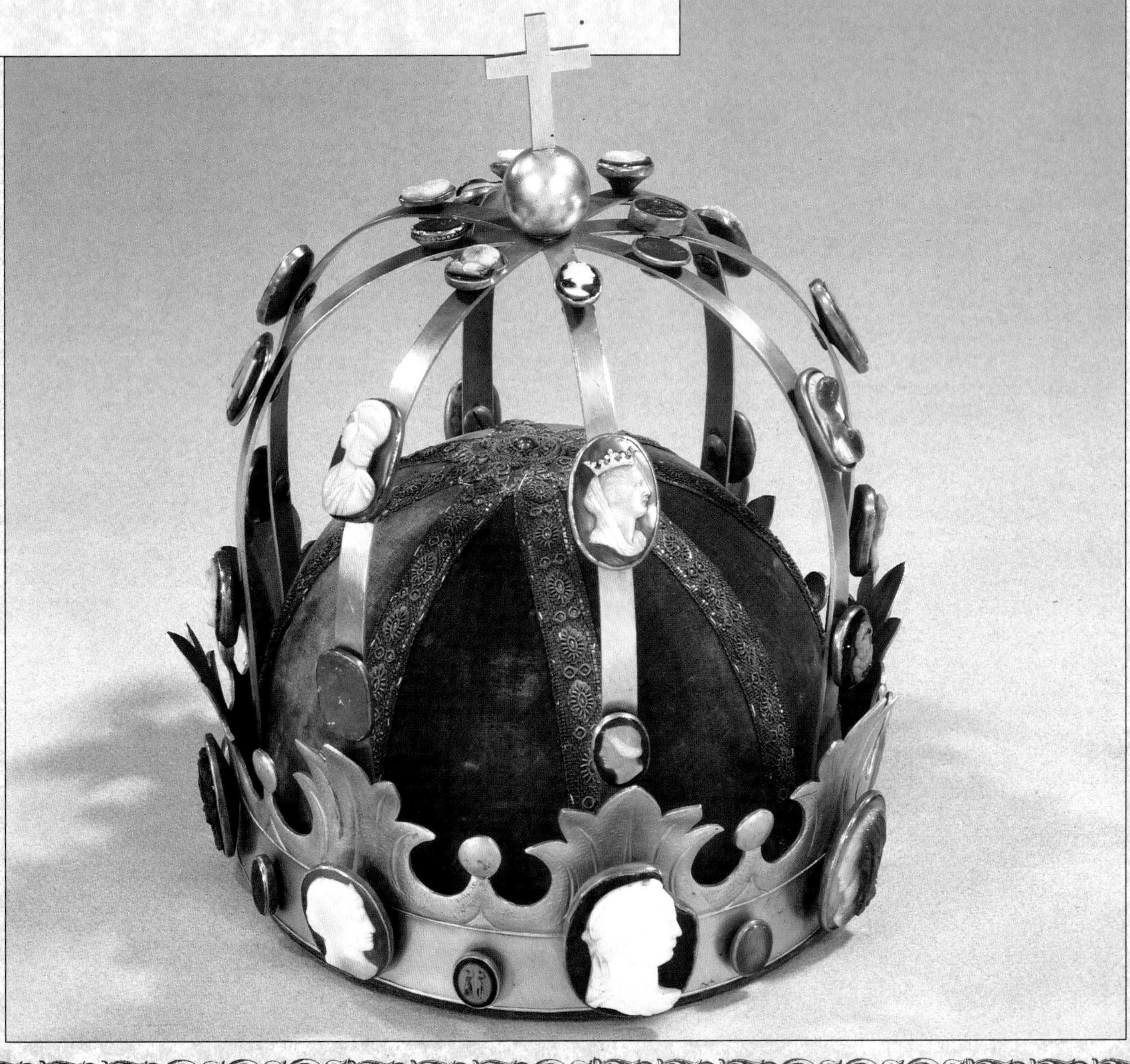

Louvre/© Photo RMN-D. Arnaudet

♔ Successful generals in Imperial Rome were rewarded with a triumphant progress through the streets of the city crowned with a wreath of laurel leaves. Napoleon's own military feats, and his enthusiasm for Julius Caesar's, led him to wear a chaplet of golden laurel leaves studded with pearls *below* to his Coronation

Woodmansterne

Versailles/© Photo RMN

♔ For his Coronation, Napoleon was dressed in a flowing, full-length white satin robe embroidered with gold. Over this he wore a cloak of crimson velvet lined with ermine and sewn with the bee motif he had chosen as the emblem of the new dynasty, to replace the fleur de lis of the Bourbons. The edges of the cloak were embroidered with intertwined leaves of olive, oak and laurel. This official portrait *right* by Gérard was made in 1805 and was one of Napoleon's favourite images of himself. Many copies were made for relatives, courtiers, and French embassies

♔ The Hand of Justice was a piece of regalia peculiar to the royal houses of France. It was carried on state occasions to symbolize the monarch's power as head of the judiciary. The Hand of Justice carried by Napoleon *below* was carved from ivory at the time of his Coronation. It was fixed to a golden shaft with a setting of gold and precious stones taken from a ring which dated from the time of Charlemagne

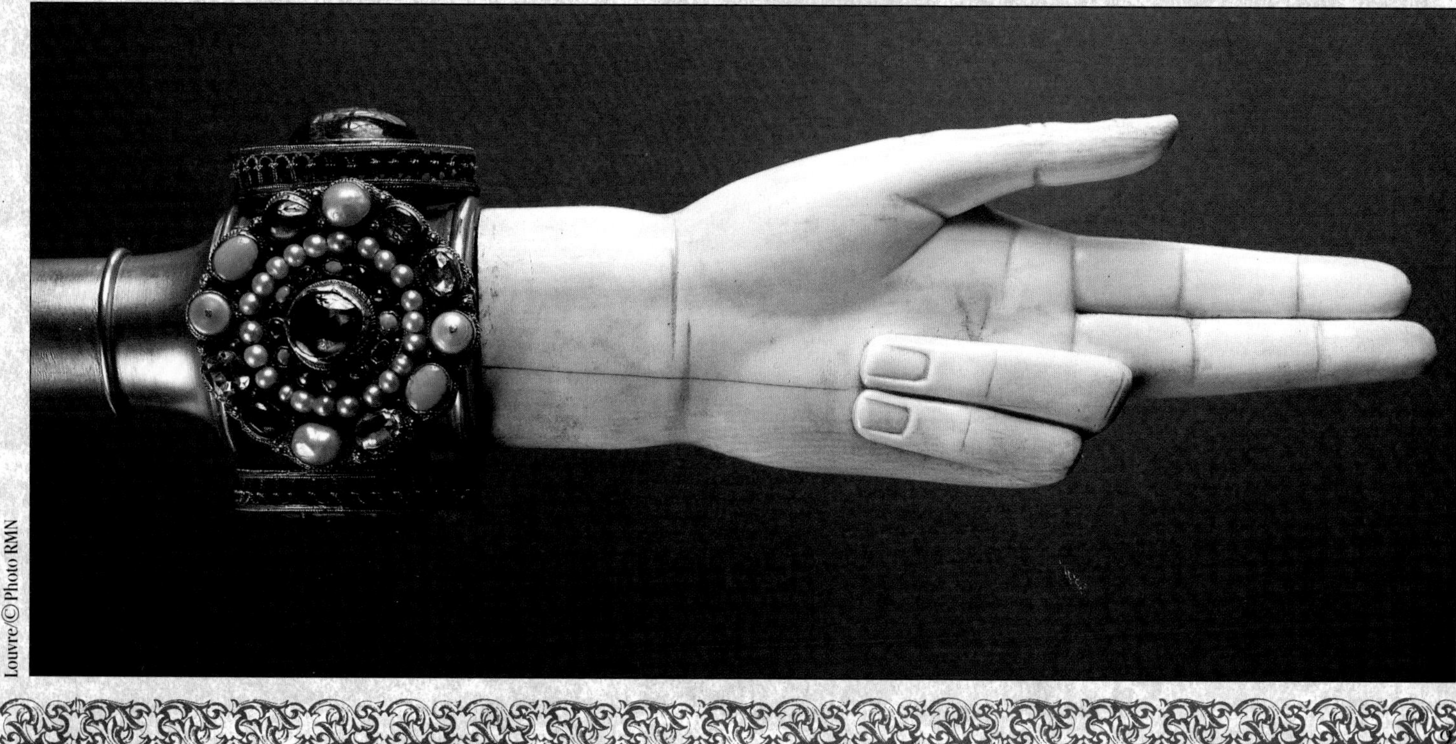

Louvre/© Photo RMN

THE EMPIRE STYLE

Josephine, almost singlehanded, created the Empire style, the flimsy, high-waisted shift dress that remained popular in Europe for a quarter of a century. Josephine first appeared in these figure-clinging garments around 1795 and with the notable Paris hostesses, Madame Tallien and Madame Récamier, began setting a fashion trend which the rest of society soon followed

♔ Josephine wears an elegant outdoor outfit in green velvet *right*. With a ruched neck and fitted sleeves ending in a slight puff, the jacket is high-waisted and decorated with a delicate white lace ruff. A jaunty white-feathered cap replaces the more conventional bonnet

♔ Josephine, portrayed here soon after her marriage to Napoleon, in a Grecian-style costume *below*. Her loosely curled, informal hairstyle is held in place by a simple, jewel-encrusted circlet. Decorating the neckline of her cream muslin gown is a gold border inset with antique cameos and precious stones

Mary Evans/Explorer

♔ The selection and purchase of her wardrobe *left* was Josephine's greatest pleasure and her principal interest in life. 'She bought everything and without ever asking the price,' commented a friend. At times her wardrobe contained as many as 676 dresses, excluding any accessories or the special costumes she kept for state occasions

Tongue-shaped, fully-lined crimson velvet train, richly embroidered in gold, with snowdrops, flowers and spiralling foliage

Simple bandeau of embossed gold, drop pearl earrings and a delicate gold and pearl necklace

Cream and gold fan to match gown

High-waisted cream silk dress with fine gold embroidery and double sleeves; a short, puff sleeve over a long fitted sleeve

The flower and foliage embroidery patterns shown here are typical Empire style

♔ On state occasions, Josephine dressed with regal but subtle elegance. Although simple in style, this gown's richness lies in the fabric, a fine silk delicately embroidered with gold *right*. It is complemented by a sumptuous velvet train. Note the striking and deliberate simplicity of Josephine's accessories

The hem, sleeves and neckline of dress have matching embroidered edging in a small repeat pattern

♔ To emphasize his dual role as heroic soldier and France's First Consul, Napoleon's dress was a mixture of military simplicity and understated richness. A flamboyant touch here *right* is the gold embroidery on breeches as well as jacket

♔ At home at Malmaison, Josephine 'almost always wore India muslin, filmy as a cloud'. Here *below* she reclines on a gold plush day bed in a see-through dress of embroidered muslin. Wearing no jewellery and with her hair swept up in the simple Grecian style, she adopts the pose of seemingly artless grace that Napoleon found so attractive.

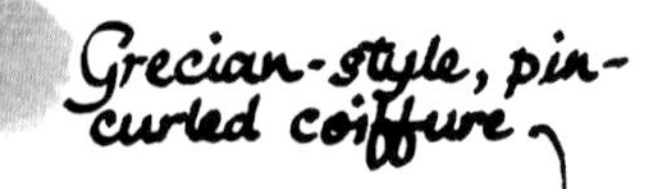

Gros: Bonaparte (detail), Musée Nat. de la Légion d'Honneur, Paris/Bridgeman/Giraudon

♔ **Josephine dressed for an evening soirée at Malmaison *right*. Both the veil and the gown, which is decorated with a wide floral border, are edged with gold. A red cashmere shawl adorns her shoulders, matching the colours of her train**

Muslin veil with gold edging worn off the face

Red cashmere shawl

♔ **As one Malmaison visitor observed, 'Nothing touched [Napoleon] like the sight of a graceful woman in a white gown. Josephine [was] well aware of this preference . . . Indeed, in general, the white dress was a uniform for the women at Malmaison.' This illustration *above* shows Josephine in the gardens of Malmaison**

Satin slippers worn with flesh-coloured tights

Skirt has a wide border of flowers, arranged into large oval shapes

'To Destiny'

When the young and fiery General Bonaparte met Josephine, he fell immediately and passionately in love with her. She, however, was intrigued but indifferent to the future Emperor of France.

Soon after their first meeting in 1795, General Bonaparte became a regular visitor left *at Josephine's house on the Rue Chantereine. He was so attentive to her that her children began to worry. They were sure that she would soon remarry and would then have much less time and love for them*

Josephine and the children continued to live in the house on the Rue Chantereine below *after her marriage. Her husband joined her there between campaigns. The house became one of the social hubs of Paris and, as her social standing increased with each new triumph for Napoleon, she lavished large amounts of care and money on it*

Hulton Picture Company

Jean-Loup Charmet

Napoleon's first meeting with Josephine arose from his role as the officer in charge of national security during the Directory. All unauthorized weapons had to be surrendered, but young Eugène de Beauharnais asked for an exception to be made of his late father's sword. The only person who could agree to this was General Bonaparte and, when he did, Josephine went to thank him. The general was soon a regular at the glamorous widow's Thursday 'at homes'.

Within weeks, 12-year-old Hortense was seated at a dinner between her mother and General Bonaparte, who, in order to talk to Josephine, 'leaned across my place so constantly and so impetuously that I was exhausted by the effort of leaning back to avoid his shoulder – and finally pulled my chair away from the table.' The General became their mother's escort to the Opera, to Barras's receptions and to soirées at the home of the Talliens. He entertained Josephine at military headquarters and drove her about in his carriage. Before long, they had exchanged portraits.

Sometime in December 1795 or January 1796, Napoleon and Josephine became lovers. After their first intimate evening together he wrote 'I awake full of you. Your portrait and the memory of the intoxication of last night have given my senses no rest. Sweet and incomparable Josephine, what is this bizarre effect you have upon my heart ... You leave at noon; in three hours I shall see you. Meanwhile, *mio dolce amor,* a thousand kisses; but do not give me any, for they set my blood on fire.'

Madame Bonaparte

Although Josephine might have preferred to have remained the mistress of the most promising young general in the army, a role which would have left her with more independence and more time for her beloved children, Napoleon insisted on marriage.

She resisted the idea at first. Although he amused her and inspired great affection, she did not love him as passionately as he loved her. Moreover, the very force of his love alarmed her. A man who fell so absolutely in love might fall out of it just as easily.

When she gave in to him and agreed to marry, her lawyer was horrified. She could have had her pick of more mature and certainly wealthier men but had agreeed to marry a young man with 'nothing but his cape and sword'. Far from being offended at the lawyer's advice, which he overheard, Napoleon was very impressed and amused by its honesty, and in any case Josephine ignored it. Her infallible instincts told her that this fiancé was a winner.

On 9 March 1796 Napoleon Bonaparte and Madame de Beauharnais were married in a short, civic ceremony. The bride, who was 32, changed her age to 28, and the groom gallantly added 18 months to his actual age to make it the same as hers. Her wedding band was inscribed with the words 'To Destiny'. The beginnings of that destiny made Napoleon two hours late for his wedding. He was delayed by a tactics meeting for his latest appointment as Commander-in-Chief of the French army that was about to conquer Italy.

The rest of the wedding party arrived at the dingy registry office on the Rue d'Antin promptly at 8pm. Lovely in a white tunic dress, with a gold fillet restraining her chestnut curls, Josephine waited impatiently for the groom with Barras, Tallien and her legal adviser.

Napoleon finally arrived with his aide-de-camp, Le Marois, at 10pm. At 10.30, the bride and groom climbed into the carriage that would take them to their house in the Rue Chantereine, where they would spend their brief honeymoon.

Early obstacles

On the day after their wedding the couple visited Josephine's children at their schools to reassure them of their importance in the new household. Although the course of Napoleon's love for Josephine seldom ran smooth, his affection for Eugène and Hortense was consistently genuine and they both acknowledged him as an exemplary stepfather.

Josephine's beloved little dog, Fortuné, was more of an obstacle to the newlyweds' happiness, for he would not relinquish his place in his mistress's bed and bit her new husband in the leg. Josephine's attachment to Fortuné was understandable because, while she was in prison, the dog had regularly trotted by the guards with messages from her children and friends tucked under his collar.

After a honeymoon of just 36 hours Napoleon hastened away to war. On his way to the

Napoleon was never under any illusions about his future wife's past. Josephine* right *was a woman of the world, and her teenage children made it impossible for her to disguise her age. It was perhaps a mark of Napoleon's need to put a special claim on her that she came to be known by everyone as Josephine, his special name for her

Malmaison/E.T. Archive

'To live for Josephine, that is the story of my life'

NAPOLEON

A JAUNDICED VIEW

To his enemies, Napoleon's alliance with Josephine was a rich source of ridicule. An 1805 cartoon *below* by the English satirist Gillray shows Napoleon peeking through a curtain as Josephine and Thérèse Tallien dance abandonedly for a drunken and bloated Paul Barras. The legend below it suggests that Barras, tired of Josephine, had offered Napoleon a promotion to take her off his hands

Andrew Edmunds, London

de Dragons, et de Rose claire Desvergers de Sanois, son épouse.

Moi, Charles Théodore François Leclercq, officier public de l'état civil du deuxième arrondissement du Canton de Paris, après avoir fait lecture, présence des parties et témoins, 1° de l'acte de naissance de Napolione Bonaparte qui constate qu'il est né le cinq février mil sept cent soixante huit, de légitime mariage de Charles Bonaparte et de Letizia Ramolini; 2° l'acte de naissance de Marie Joseph Rose de Tascher, qui constate qu'elle est née le vingt trois juin mil sept cent soixante sept, de légitime mariage de Joseph Gaspard de Tascher et de Rose claire Desvergers de Sanois; Vu l'extrait de décès de Alexandre François Marie Beauharnais, qui constate qu'il est décédé le cinq thermidor an deux, mari à Marie Joseph Rose de Tascher; Vu l'extrait des publications dud. mariage, duement affiché le temps prescrit par la loi, sans opposition; et après aussi que Napolione Bonaparte et Marie Joseph Rose de Tascher ont eu déclaré à haute voix se prendre mutuellement pour époux, j'ai prononcé à haute voix que Napolione Bonaparte et Marie Joseph Rose de Tascher sont unis en mariage, et ce, présence des témoins majeurs ci-après nommés, savoir: Paul Barras, membre du Directoire exécutif, domicilié Palais du Luxembourg; Jean Lemarois, aide de camp, capitaine, domicilié rue des Capucines; Jean Lambert Talien, membre du corps législatif, domicilié à Chaillot; Etienne Jacques Jérôme Calmelet, homme de loi, domicilié rue de la place Vendôme N° 207, qui tous ont signé avec les parties et moi, après lecture./.

M. J. R. Tascher

Napolione Buonaparte

DON. N° 2292

Tallien Pr. Barras Leclerq J. Lemarois Calmelet

♔ *At their civic marriage ceremony, Josephine signed the Act of Marriage* above *in her maiden name, M. J. R. Tascher, while Napoleon used the Corsican form, Napoleone Buonoparte*

♔ *The ceremony itself* below *was a simple one, conducted by a minor official in an upstairs room in what had once been an hotel. No family members were present*

front he stopped off in Nice to tell his mother about his marriage. The Bonaparte family did not disguise their disappointment with the marriage. This relatively poor widow, six years older than Napoleon and with two children and a decidedly risqué past, was not worthy of the darling of their family.

The incomparable Josephine

In Italy Napoleon put his military master plan into action. Inspired by his leadership, the conscript French army overcame their enemy's two-to-one numerical superiority in a series of battles which culminated with victory and a brilliant treaty. In the midst of this spectacular campaign Napoleon was obsessed with his 'gentle and incomparable Josephine'. Alone in his tent at night he wept over her portrait. 'Scarcely have we been married, scarcely have we been united, and already we are separated . . .' He wrote to her every day, sometimes more than once. Courier after courier arrived at Josephine's Paris house with these ink-blotched, delirious love letters.

Even by contemporary standards, these letters make for a passionate read – in the prudish 19th century, when they were first published, the constant references to sex had to be censored. Napoleon sent his 'thousand and one kisses' to every single part of his wife's anatomy, to her eyes and her arms, her throat and her lips, her breasts 'and lower, much lower', 'everywhere'.

Napoleon repeatedly asked his political masters for permission for Josephine to join him. When the Directory eventually gave this permission it was a reward to their star general.

But, as Napoleon burned in passionate, wistful expectation, Josephine seemed in no hurry to join him. Early in May he accidentally dropped the miniature portrait of Josephine that he always carried. Napoleon, like his wife, was very superstitious. As he stooped to pick up the shattered glass, he said to General Marmont 'Either my wife is ill or she is being unfaithful.'

Napoleon was enormously relieved when he was told that pregnancy was delaying his wife's departure from Paris. The arduous journey would threaten her health, as well as that of the eagerly awaited child, and so he urged her not to move. But in June there was a miscarriage, or at least a gynaecological mishap which made it necessary for three doctors to visit Josephine, and soon afterwards Napoleon began to expect to see his wife again. But she would not leave Paris. Napoleon became frantic and Josephine, who failed to respond to his love letters satisfactorily, was evasive.

In Paris she enjoyed public acclaim for her husband's victories. Madame Bonaparte was honoured as Napoleon's lucky mascot, as 'Notre Dame de Victoires' and was automatically the 'first lady' at victory celebrations. She was well suited to this role, knowing how to dress for the part and how to accept the good wishes of jubilant crowds graciously.

The name of the street where Napoleon and Josephine lived was changed to Rue de la Victoire. From school, Hortense complained about the celebrity's life her mother was leading. 'I suppose it is the general's victories that keep you from coming. If that is what deprives me of my chère petite maman's visits, I'll start hoping for an end to victories.'

Josephine's infatuation

It was neither fame nor pregnancy, but a suave young hussar by the name of Hippolyte Charles that kept Josephine from joining her lovesick husband in Italy. In time Josephine would love Napoleon as passionately as he loved her, but in the first year of her marriage she seems to have simply liked him. It was different with Charles, who was unequivocally handsome, very dashing and full of style and wit. He temporarily made a reluctant bride of Madame Bonaparte.

Infatuated with her hussar, Josephine was reluctant to set out on the two-week journey to Milan. She delayed and delayed until Napoleon was nearly demented with anguish. It was July when she finally arrived in Milan.

Although it took him three days of travelling from another part of Italy to meet the wife he had not seen since March, Napoleon was not disappointed by the reunion. His Josephine was still incomparable. 'Once reunited with his wife at Milan,' General Marmont wrote, 'General Bonaparte was supremely happy, for he lived then solely for her. And so it was for a long time; a love so true, so pure, so exclusive had never possessed the heart of a man, and that man of so superior an order.'

'I only win battles; Josephine wins hearts for me.'

NAPOLEON

When military duties called Napoleon away a week later, he wrote back to Josephine. 'A few days ago I thought I loved you, but now, since I have seen you again I love you a thousand times more. Everyday since I met you I have loved you more....'

Although supremely gratified by her husband's love – especially his long-distance solicitude for her children – Josephine was still put out by his devotion. 'My husband doesn't love me – he worships me! I am afraid he will go mad with love.' Nevertheless, she obliged her 'tenderest of lovers' by agreeing to join him at Brescia in northern Italy.

A fortuitous premonition

The governor of Brescia, who was secretly allied to the Austrians, had invited the Bonapartes to a special reception. If Josephine had not had a remarkable premonition, and persuaded her husband to leave Brescia almost as soon as she had arrived, they could both have been captured by the Austrians. From Verona,

At the end of the 18th century, about the time of his marriage, Napoleon's image was in the process of changing. The romantic, aquiline hero with flowing hair, seen in an unfinished portrait by David below, ***began to give way to a more rounded, statesmanlike figure***

David: Unfinished Portrait of Napoleon (detail), Louvre/Bridgeman/Giraudon

Lecomte: Josephine at Lake Garda, Malmaison/Lauros-Giraudon

Josephine's visit to Napoleon in northern Italy almost ended in disaster. At Lake Garda, her party was fired upon by Austrian gunboats above. ***Two of the carriage horses fell dead between their traces, and one of the escorting cavalrymen was killed by a shell fragment. Josephine escaped the turmoil in a peasant cart. When Napoleon saw her distress, he swore that 'Würmser [the Austrian general] will pay dearly for your tears'***

Napoleon sent Josephine to safety via the shore of Lake Garda, but there her entourage was fired upon by an Austrian gunboat.

This was the third time Josephine had narrowly escaped death, and she was in tears when Napoleon snatched her from the peasant's cart in which she had fled the danger. From now on the commander-in-chief's wife must stay away from the war zone, and so Napoleon at war was Napoleon without Josephine.

Whenever possible, Napoleon tried to be with his wife in Milan. Upon arriving at the palace he would dash straight into Josephine's private suite. Until he found her he was like a discontented child, and once beside her he would fondle her with a lack of inhibition that amused and sometimes embarrassed the other people present. The financier, Hamelin, remembered how he played with Josephine 'like a child, teasing her until he made her cry, caressing her so boldly, so heartily that I considered it best to walk away to the window and pretend to be checking on the weather.'

It was from this atmosphere of wedded bliss that Josephine wrote to tell Aunt Edmée that she could not have a better husband. But he was away for much of the time and she was often bored. She also missed her children. This was partly remedied by Eugène's arrival in Milan as his stepfather's aide-de-camp.

In the summer of 1797 Napoleon's family descended on Milan for his sister Pauline's wedding to General Leclerc. The arrangements were made by Josephine, and since the event

THE ITALIAN CAMPAIGN

Napoleon became Commander in Chief of the Army of Italy in March 1796. Morale was low when he joined his men, who were hard pressed by the Austrians, but he led them to a series of stunning victories, capturing enemy flags *right* and thousands of men as they rampaged across northern Italy. The 10-month campaign took them within 75 miles of Vienna before the Austrians made peace. Bonaparte's position as a hero of France was assured

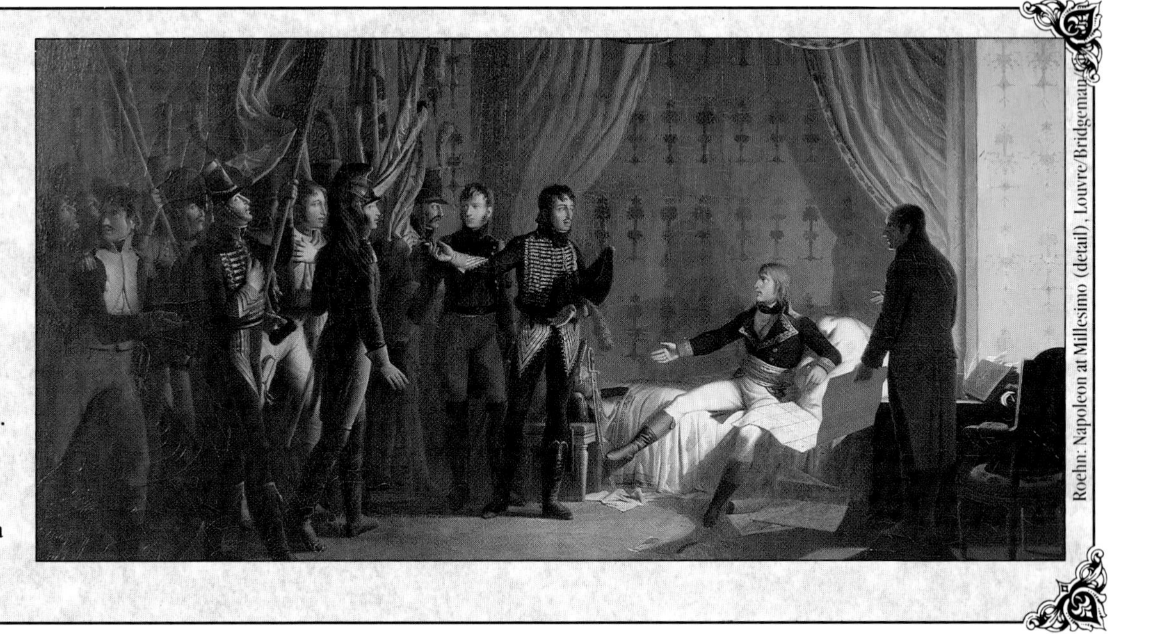

Roehn: Napoleon at Millesimo (detail), Louvre/Bridgeman

Beautiful and flirtatious, Pauline Bonaparte above *first married General Leclerc, and then the fabulously wealthy Prince Camillo Borghese*

Napoleon's first formal portrait, by Gros, was painted in 1796 in Milan. It shows him above *in the thick of the fighting at the Battle of Arcola*

Napoleon's military successes put his political star very much in the ascendant. Josephine settled into a new public role below *with an easy grace*

was an opportunity to cultivate the Bonapartes it was unfortunate that she did not get on with the bride. Pauline Bonaparte was 17, very beautiful and very vain. The sculptor Canova used her as a model of female beauty and in later life she liked to display herself by bathing nude in front of her ladies-in-waiting.

Pauline's revenge

Almost inevitably, the most attractive of the Bonaparte sisters was arrogant, and she blamed her sister-in-law for the abrupt way in which her unsuitable relationship with an older married man had been broken off. Although it was Napoleon who had arranged for her to marry General Leclerc, Pauline found it more convenient to resent Josephine. After she married she got ammunition for revenge. As Madame Leclerc she found out about Josephine's affair with Captain Charles, who was attached to her husband's retinue.

But this storm cloud was still only on the horizon. It seemed that Josephine's reckless ways with money threatened General Bonaparte's love for her more than the spite of her in-laws. He finally arrived back in Paris to be presented with the bill for the decoration of the conjugal home. It came to three times the value of the actual house, which, in view of the scale of Josephine's vision, was hardly surprising. The master bedroom, for example, was fit for any returning conqueror, with the drum-style occasional tables and the twin beds mounted on cannon, which sprung together at the pull of a lever.

Despite Napoleon's strictures, Josephine had also done little to curtail her extravagance over clothes, jewellery and other finery. Napoleon was deeply displeased.

Bourgain: Napoleon's Entry into Cairo Fine Art Photographic Library

♔ ***Following his successes against the Austrians in Italy, Bonaparte, who had always been fascinated by the Orient, was sent to Egypt by the Directory in 1798, with the aim of cutting off British trade routes and ending their influence in the Middle East. He landed on 1 July. After an overwhelming victory at the Battle of the Pyramids on 21 July, Napoleon entered Cairo in triumph*** above. ***A year later, naval defeats, rebellions and plague had so weakened the French army's position that Napoleon returned to France and his political destiny***

Napoleon had been ordered home from the Rhineland by the Directors, who wished his presence at a victory ball in Paris.

The victory ball

At the ball the famous bluestocking Madame de Staël accosted Napoleon to ask him what kind of women most aroused his admiration. She made no secret of her passion for Napoleon and her bafflement at his obsession with a 'bland beauty' like Josephine. She had tried to convince him that, with her intellect and his 'destiny,' they made a perfect couple. Madame Bonaparte was beside her husband and heard him telling Madame de Staël that he most admired women who produced a lot of children. While this may have put Madame de Staël in her place, it was hardly a remark welcomed by Josephine, who had so far failed to produce any Bonaparte children.

STORM CLOUDS

Soon after, Josephine weathered the first storm about Captain Charles. A maid who had been dismissed took her revenge by telling her former master the compromising details of Josephine's route to Italy: Josephine had travelled with Captain Charles for much of the journey and had met him regularly there.

Josephine calmed her husband by challenging the maid's own morality and integrity, and by simply denying everything. He accepted her denials, but the incident, combined with the insinuations of Pauline Leclerc, must have given him an uneasy feeling. Captain Charles resigned – or was forced to resign – from the army, so that officially his path no longer crossed that of the Bonapartes. As Pauline crowed, 'My sister-in-law nearly died of grief. I consoled my brother, who was very unhappy.'

In the spring of 1798 the conqueror of Italy had more than Captain Charles on his mind. He had decided to confront France's outstanding enemy, Britain. By occupying Egypt he would cut Britain off from India. Napoleon brought Josephine with him to Toulon in order to put off their 'cruel parting' until he set sail for Egypt in May. She was despatched to take the waters at Plombières, fabled for their help with infertility. After two years of marriage without a child, she was more vulnerable to Bonaparte family jibes, and at 35, time for an heir was running out.

'I consoled my brother, who was very unhappy.'

PAULINE BONAPARTE ON JOSEPHINE'S INFIDELITY

In Egypt, Napoleon learned conclusive details of his wife's infidelity with Charles. Apparently, it was General Junot who took it upon himself to enlighten his chief, and Napoleon treated his confidences seriously.

For the first time the word 'divorce' was heard on Napoleon's lips, but he was still more miserable and hurt than outraged. To his elder brother Joseph he wrote 'My emotions are spent, withered. Glory stales. At the age of 29 I have exhausted everything; life has nothing more to offer.' In the same mail pouch there was a letter from Eugène to his mother, warning her of what was being said about her.

Mocked for being a cuckold, Napoleon risked losing his dignity, and possibly the all-important esteem of his soldiers. He immediately ordered a selection of beautiful Egyptian women to be brought before him so that he could choose a mistress. But he dismissed all six of the women as too fat.

Choosing a mistress

As he confided in a member of his staff, his ideal woman was a tall, 'slender and graceful' creature dressed in the palest of gowns. He liked to imagine such a woman walking along shadowy garden paths. In other words, a substitute for Josephine had to be found.

Pauline Fourès was slim, blonde and 20, with a reputation for liveliness and wit. Almost as soon as she had been introduced to Napoleon, he contrived to spill wine on her dress and they went upstairs to clean it up, rejoining the dinner party much later, to ribald applause.

Meanwhile, her unfortunate husband, sent on some suitably faraway mission, was captured by the British, who gleefully sent him back to Napoleon's headquarters.

Peace in Paris

When she heard that her alienated husband had landed in France, Josephine hastened to get to him before his family, and before the resolution to divorce her had hardened. Because he took a different route, she managed to miss him. He reached their home in Paris to find the shutters drawn and his wife absent. When told that she had left to meet him he shrugged. That night he stormed about in a terrible rage. He swore that he would tear his own heart out and throw it on the fire, and the suggestion that he might forgive her enraged him further.

Though his anger suggested that he still loved Josephine, Napoleon's all-important dignity was threatened by the scandal. It was on that level that he was most vulnerable to the advice of his family, who passionately denounced 'la putana' (the whore). Josephine, whose absence was construed as guilt, came back to Paris to find her personal possessions in trunks at the gate and the door bolted against her. For hours she tearfully pleaded with her husband to be let in, but only after she begged for admission hand-in-hand with Eugène and Hortense did Napoleon give in.

Much later, Napoleon said that he had not wanted the children to suffer on account of their mother's faults, but in view of what happened next morning it must be concluded that Josephine still moved him. His brother, Lucien, when admitted to the marital bedroom found a smiling Napoleon and Josephine having breakfast in bed. She had persuaded him that the worst of the accusations made against her were untrue. But although she had won this round, she could no longer take her husband's absolute love for granted.

♔ ***When he was in Egypt, news of his wife's infidelity led Napoleon to seek a mistress. One place he looked was in Cairo's Tivoli Garden*** **above,** ***where French officers and their wives gathered.***

♔ ***Despite the early problems of their marriage, Napoleon kept faith with Josephine*** **below** ***in his heart***

ROYAL RESIDENCE

MALMAISON

The chateau of Malmaison, on the outskirts of Paris, was built in 1622 on the site of a former leper house (*mala mansio*). Josephine acquired the property in 1799 and employed the leading Empire architects, Charles Percier and Pierre François Fontaine, to extend and restore it. Josephine and Napoleon spent the happiest moments of their life in this country retreat

This gracious chateau below *served as the summer residence of Napoleon and Josephine. Here they often entertained informally, making particular use of the splendid gardens, the design of which, with walks, temples and grottoes, Josephine personally supervised*

The Music Room right *was a favourite with Josephine who played the harp and whose instrument, decorated with a golden eagle, can be seen in the room today. The room was also much used by Hortense de Beauharnais who was an accomplished pianist and composer*

E.T. Archive

© Photo RMN

Josephine's Bedchamber was on the first floor, along with the other private apartments. Her magnificent bed of carved wood painted with gold leaf right *is the work of Jacob Desmalter, the craftsman responsible for most of the furniture in Malmaison. Josephine died in this very bed at Malmaison on 29 May 1814*

The Entrance Hall below *was reached from the courtyard via a tent-like porch. With its black-and-white checkered marble floor, stately columns and busts of Napoleon's family, it was here that distinguished guests from Paris gathered before making their way to the Dining Room or one of the grand salons on the ground floor of the chateau*

© Photo RMN

© Photo RMN

© Photo RMN

Lauros-Giraudon

♔ *The Salon Doré (Golden Room)* above *on the ground floor was decorated principally in white and gold, Napoleon's and Josephine's favourite colours. The gold-painted and richly upholstered furniture is typical of the opulent Empire style. The sphinx, seen here on the chairs, was a popular decorative motif with Napoleon since it commemorated his conquest of the Nile in 1798*

♔ *This richly embroidered fabric* left *was part of the decoration of Josephine's bedroom. The swan design in the centre of the panel was particularly associated with the Empress and it appears on many pieces of furniture made specially for her*

♔ ***Josephine's 'everyday' boudoir*** **above** ***is remarkable for its simplicity and elegance. The wooden bed, embellished with a pair of golden swans, is enclosed in a mirrored recess and draped in the colours which were her trademark – white and gold. Despite its apparent plainness, everything is of the most exquisite workmanship***

♔ ***Napoleon's taste for plain colours, dark wood furniture and tent-like drapes can be seen in his bedchamber*** **left** ***at Malmaison. Although one of the least opulent rooms in the chateau, classical symbols celebrating honour, patriotism and victory typically decorate the room of the French Emperor***

♔ ***Napoleon complained that The Library*** **above** ***reminded him of a church vestry. Its curious design by Jacob Desmalter was dictated by the presence of a chimney flue from the kitchen below which could not be got rid of nor repositioned. Desmalter, with great ingenuity, concealed it behind mirrored columns***

FORGING AN EMPIRE

View of Malmaison/E.T. Archive

DURING THIS PERIOD OF CALM IN THEIR RELATIONSHIP, NAPOLEON AND JOSEPHINE DREW CLOSER. THEY SOON DISCOVERED THE STRENGTH OF THEIR MUTUAL DEPENDENCE, AS THEY PREPARED FOR THEIR ASCENT TO THE THRONE.

After their reconciliation the Bonapartes were happier than they had been during the first four years of their marriage. But what now endeared Josephine to Napoleon was not so much her supple body as the way in which she imprinted her relaxed, gentle personality on his domestic life. Considering the stresses and strains attached to being the military genius of Europe, and the violence of his temper, her success as a calming influence on the volatile Napoleon was no mean achievement.

Josephine's presence

Everyone close to the couple observed that they still preferred to share a bedroom and that whenever possible they ate together. After hours discussing military tactics, Napoleon was relieved by Josephine's chatter. On a whim, he would sometimes leave his study in order to visit his wife's apartments, which he reached via a private staircase. But if other people were with her, he would scowl and turn on his heel. After working late, he liked nothing better than to have Josephine come to his study to read to him in her low, melodious voice. On grand occasions he enjoyed helping her choose an outfit, and commented on her toilette.

Although Josephine's excessive spending on clothes was the major cause of arguments with Napoleon, he did appreciate its results. She always looked stunning and again and again he acknowledged 'all the charm' that his stylish wife lent to his intimate life. Nowhere was that charm more in evidence than at Malmaison, and Bonaparte looked forward to weekends there like an eager schoolboy looking forward to his holidays.

During the Egyptian campaign, and the

Malmaison* above, *the chateau just outside Paris that Josephine bought soon after her marriage to Napoleon. It was the scene of their happiest times together

Josephine* right *at Malmaison, dressed in one of the flimsy, clinging gowns that Napoleon loved to see her in

Napoleon, Josephine and her attendants enjoy the enchantment of Malmaison* below*. 'Nowhere, except perhaps upon the field of battle, have I seen Bonaparte more happy than in his gardens at Malmaison,' wrote his secretary

Viger du Vigneau: "La Rose" of Malmaison (detail), Lauros/Giraudon

'Nothing touched Napoleon like the sight of a graceful woman in a white gown.'

GENERAL JUNOT'S WIFE

Ingres: Napoleon Bonaparte, Musée des Beaux-Arts, Liege/Bridgeman Art Library

This portrait of Napoleon was painted soon after he became First Consul and the most powerful man in France

marital crisis, Josephine had purchased Malmaison, a country house set in 300 acres of lawn, woods and farmland just ten miles down the Seine from Paris. As it later turned out, the purchase of Malmaison was a shrewd investment in the survival of Josephine's marriage because this house was the scene of her happiest days with Napoleon.

The Malmaison idyll

When Napoleon had fantasized about an elegant woman gliding down a fragrant garden pathway he might have been imagining his wife at Malmaison. Although he increased the size of the estate by buying more land around Malmaison, Josephine was responsible for the estate's landscaping; garden paths wound round pools, fountains, flowering meadows, follies and miniature temples, a menagerie and even a replica of a Swiss village with a resident cowherd. The brilliant blooms of Martinique were not forgotten in the hothouses, and exotic birds occupied the aviaries. The interior of the house was totally refurbished to Josephine's taste, in the clean classical lines that became known as the Empire style. Her place at table in the dining room was marked by a rose in the mosaic floor, and the door of her husband's study was painted with martial motifs.

Malmaison was a family home, which high society visited only by invitation. Whenever possible, Napoleon and Josephine, Eugène and Hortense, as well as his younger brothers and sisters gathered there. In fine weather they enjoyed boisterous outdoor games, and dined al fresco. Afterwards Napoleon and Josephine would stroll together in the gardens. In less fine weather, there were card games and billiards, ghost stories and concerts, as well as enthusiastic amateur productions in the specially built little theatre. For Paris society, the Sunday night ball at Malmaison was the key event of the week. White was almost regulation dress for the ladies, and Josephine enjoyed making a sensational entrance. On one occasion Napoleon proudly led her to the centre of the dance floor in a gown made of hundreds of pale pink rose petals stitched to shimmering white satin.

The First Consul

By 1799 all sections of French society were profoundly dissatisfied with the lacklustre Directory, and they looked to their brilliant general for an alternative government. Later in that year he engineered the coup that gave political power to three consuls, of which he was the senior First Consul. Early on a December morning Napoleon returned to his anxious wife in the Rue de la Victoire to tell her, 'Tomorrow we sleep in the Luxembourg.'

LOYAL BEAUHARNAIS

In the Imperial court, there were few young men more loyal, kindhearted and devoted than Josephine's son, Eugène de Beauharnais. To his mother he was always solicitous and protective, more like a brother than a son. To Napoleon, he was a fond stepson and, as a 16-year-old boy, had accompanied the General to Egypt.

Eugène pointedly refused any compensation for his loss of position as vice-chancellor of state after the divorce of Napoleon and Josephine, disarming Napoleon with his obvious sincerity and unselfishness, in marked contrast with the grasping, ambitious Bonaparte family.

Isabey: Prince Eugène, Cabinet des Arts Graphique, Louvre © Photo RMN

Dutiful as ever, Eugène acquiesced in the marriage Napoleon imperiously arranged for him with Princess Augusta of Bavaria. Surprisingly, the marriage, which blossomed into a love match, was extremely happy

Richard: Hortense de Beauharnais (detail), Lauros-Giraudon

♔ ***Hortense de Beauharnais*** left, ***Josephine's daughter, who at 18 was persuaded into a loveless marriage with Louis Bonaparte, Napoleon's brother. After producing three children, she separated from and finally divorced Louis who had been created King of Holland by Napoleon. Throughout her life, Hortense remained devoted and loyal to both Josephine and Napoleon***

Although too much the military man to have a great personal taste for pomp, Napoleon realized that the relatively austere Directory had not been popular. Provided it was more democratically available, the people liked 'la gloire' and with the help of his elegant wife he would provide it. Accordingly, the move to the Tuileries was marked by a magnificent formal procession, with rows of carriages and soldiers saluting as Napoleon and Josephine entered the palace of Louis XVI and Marie-Antoinette. Letizia, or Madame Mère, as she was officially known, wept at the sight of her son's eminence.

'Come little Creole, step into the bed of your masters.'

NAPOLEON TO JOSEPHINE

After dinner on that day Napoleon picked Josephine up and carried her off to the massive state bed, which had been placed in their bedroom, 'Come little Creole, step into the bed of your masters.'

Once in firm control of executive power Napoleon acted swiftly to stabilize the situation in Europe. After a second Italian campaign he conclusively defeated the Austrians at the Battle of Marengo. A temporarily effective peace deal was also made with the pro-French Tsar Paul, while Prussia, Denmark and Sweden joined together in the League of Armed Neutrality, which was designed to isolate Napoleon's chief remaining enemy, Britain, by blocking her trade with continental Europe. These arrangements resulted in a period of comparative peace between 1800 and 1803, during which Napoleon concentrated on the domestic reforms that were his most lasting achievement.

The Consular household

In 1802 Napoleon became First Consul for life, with the power to nominate his own successor. Already, he was the emperor of France in all but name, and the Consular household was effectively France's court. Josephine excelled at presiding over the new arrangements, knowing how to receive foreign ambassadors, even foreign royalty, discreetly and graciously. Tact was all-important because émigrés, who had fled during the revolution, returned to Paris in great numbers and the dignitaries assembled for particular occasions could have embarrassingly different backgrounds.

Napolean was also mindful of the importance of his household as a national example. As he put it in a letter to Josephine: 'Grandeur has its price – an Empress cannot live like an ordinary citizen.' Josephine could wear the crown jewels but her personal waywardness in financial matters was now strictly controlled, as she lived more in the public gaze.

♔ ***This charming portrait of Josephine in the woods of Malmaison*** below ***captures something of her wistful attraction and graceful style. Gifted with exquisite taste and an unaffected elegance and charm, she overcame her lack of conventional beauty to become one of the most captivating women of her time. Napoleon said of her after her death, 'She was a woman in every sense of the word, vivid, vivacious and . . . tenderhearted'***

Prud'hon: Josephine (detail), Louvre/© Photo RMN

Hulton Picture Company

On 18 May 1804 Napoleon was proclaimed 'emperor of the Republic' above by a unanimous Senate. It was a title he preferred to that of king, finding it 'grander, and more stirring'

The intricate Coronation ritual was planned down to the last detail by Napoleon and Josephine* below. *The great artists and craftsmen of the day were brought in to advise not only on the official costumes but also to plan and direct the Coronation procession and decoration of Notre Dame cathedral

The more successful Napoleon was as the First Consul, the more pressure there was for an heir. Various attempts made on his life only highlighted the fact that there was no obvious Bonaparte to succeed him, nor, in spite of Josephine's repeated visits to Plombières, would there be.

The sacrifice of Hortense

In desperation she turned to her pretty and talented daughter, of whom Napoleon was inordinately fond. If Hortense de Beauharnais were to marry the 23-year-old Louis Bonaparte, a son of theirs might serve as the First Consul's heir.

Although Hortense had always believed in marrying only for love, she bowed to pressure from her mother to marry the silent, serious Louis. They made an unhappy couple and years later Louis wrote, 'We were both equally victims of an unjust and false policy.' But by 1802 Hortense had produced the requisite son. Hortense's baby relieved, rather than removed the pressure for an heir, and so Josephine became more preoccupied with other ways of safeguarding her own marriage, which a growing number of people openly spoke of as being against the national interest.

Jean-Loup Charmet

The Coronation

Late in 1804 Napoleon, who had squashed a royalist conspiracy against his rule, was hailed by the senate as Emperor of the French. This move surprised no one, though it disappointed those who hoped that the self-made Corsican soldier would disdain the trappings of monarchy. By the end of November Pope Pius VII had arrived in Paris to perform the ceremony.

'Josephine would have shared my misfortune. It is right for her to share my success.'

NAPOLEON

At nine o'clock on the morning of 2 December 1804 a great golden coach, drawn by eight bay horses and surmounted by a crown and four spread-winged imperial eagles, passed through the gates of the Tuileries. Inside sat Napoleon in the crimson velvet which would be exchanged for imperial robes at Notre Dame, and Josephine, glittering with 2000 diamonds, wearing a gown of white satin embroidered in gold and silver. According to a reliable witness, Josephine rose to this august occasion by looking not a day over 25, while Napoleon's face, especially his profile, looked like that on an ancient Greek coin.

Although he listened to those, especially members of his family, who queried the advisability of giving Josephine a prominent place in the ceremony, Napoleon ignored them, 'If I had been thrown into prison instead of mounting a throne, Josephine would have shared my misfortune. It is right for her to share my success.' The Pope was not so lucky. Napoleon allowed Pius to anoint his hands and to bless him but as the old man reached for the crown of golden laurel leaves Napoleon snatched it and crowned himself the new Emperor.

David: The Coronation of Napoleon (detail), Louvre/Giraudon

Then it was Josephine's turn to advance towards the altar, her ermine-trimmed train carried with less than good grace by her Bonaparte sisters-in-law, Caroline, Pauline and Elisa. Taking great pains to make sure that the little crown sat comfortably alongside the diamond tiara on his wife's head, the Emperor crowned his Empress. But when Josephine rose from her knees the Bonaparte sisters let the heavy train fall against her, with the result that she almost staggered under its weight. Seeing this, Napoleon hissed a warning at his sisters, who duly picked it up again, as the choir and the organ struck up. Back at the Tuileries after the exhausting ceremony, Napoleon was a supremely happy man.

A family business

Napoleon's brothers and sisters did well from the Emperor's spectacular career, with the exception of Lucien, who was temporarily out of favour because, of all things, of an unsuitable relationship with a married woman. His brothers became princes and Eugène de Beauharnais, who soon made a happy marriage to a German princess, was eventually adopted as his stepfather's son.

As a result of her second marriage to Prince Borghese, Pauline Bonaparte was already a princess at the time of the coronation. But Caroline amd Elisa were piqued because, unlike their brother's wives, and Hortense in particular, they were not at first given princess status. It is said that Caroline Murat fainted with jealousy when she heard Hortense being addressed as 'Your Highness'. Napoleon could now move members of his family about Europe, from throne to throne, like pieces on a chessboard. Even so, the other Bonapartes continued to be troubled by the Emperor's special interest in Hortense's and Louis's sons – the possible heirs to the Imperial dynasty. And it was inevitable that the family should blame Josephine for Napoleon's interest.

Napoleon crowns his beloved Josephine as she raises her clasped hands towards him. General Junot's wife was an eye-witness to this very incident and noted that Josephine could not suppress her tears. For the royal couple, it was 'one of those fleeting moments of pure felicity unique in a lifetime.' David, the official painter of the Coronation, took three years to complete this painting, in which every minute detail of costume and design is recorded

Napoleon sits on the terrace of St Cloud with his nieces and nephews above. ***They include three of his sister Caroline Murat's children and two sons of the King and Queen of Holland. The boy sitting on the Emperor's knee later became Napoleon III***

Napoleon II, the King of Rome left ***was the Emperor's heir by his second wife, the Austrian Archduchess Marie-Louise***

The infant heir above ***was named Napoleon Francis Charles Joseph. His father-emperor died when he was ten***

Family Album

The Bonaparte and Beauharnais children

Gerard: Eugène de Beauharnais, Versailles/© Photo RMN

♔ ***Eugène de Beauharnais*** above, ***Josephine's son, became Viceroy of Italy and was proclaimed a royal prince by Napoleon***

♔ ***Hortense de Beauharnais, Queen of Holland*** above ***Josephine's daughter by her first marriage, became the wife of Napoleon's unstable brother Louis. Their son inherited the French Empire***

Gros: Queen Hortense and her son, Musée des Beaux-Arts/Jean Loup Charmet

♔ ***Hortense*** right ***with her son Louis, who became President of France in 1848 and Emperor Napoleon III four years later. Napoleon's own son died too young to inherit the title***

TEARS AND JEALOUSY

ALTHOUGH STILL DEVOTED TO HIS WIFE, NAPOLEON'S NEED FOR DISTRACTIONS LED HIM INTO THE ARMS OF MANY DIFFERENT WOMEN. HIS INFIDELITIES, TOGETHER WITH HIS OBSESSIONAL DESIRE FOR AN HEIR, TORE JOSEPHINE APART

FROM THE CORONATION ONWARDS THE EMPEROR SLEPT less frequently with his wife. At St Cloud, his rooms were some distance from hers and he reached them after a conspicuous walk down a long passage behind a torch-bearing valet. As a result, the whole court knew the level of the imperial couple's intimacy and Josephine, who became anxious about these nocturnal visits, was in high spirits when Napoleon chose to come to her bed: 'We had a wonderful night – he was as ardent as a young lieutenant.' Napoleon loved her as he had loved no one else, but he was no longer totally dependent on her.

La Grassini

During the second Italian campaign, in 1800, Napoleon re-encountered Madame Grassini, the prima donna of the Scala Opera in Milan. This golden-voiced lady had previously tried to attract her powerful fan's erotic interest, but without success. This time, however, he did respond. An invitation to Paris, which amounted to a royal command, followed this Italian adventure, and La Grassini was set up in a house there at Napoleon's expense. When gossip about the affair reached Josephine she employed spies, usually the servants of friends, to record the number and duration of the meetings between the singer and her husband. But La Grassini, who had achieved more of a presence in Napoleon's life than Pauline Fourès, soon escaped from her gilded cage by eloping with a violinist. She had discovered that everywhere but in bed, Napoleon belonged to his wife, and in bed he was not the most accomplished of lovers.

With Josephine, Napoleon was unusually considerate and gentle; his other women were less fortunate. In exile on St Helena (1815 – 1821) he himself said that he came into season 'like a dog' and sexually he lacked finesse. Concerned mainly with his own pleasure, he preferred passive, undemanding lovers. Often, Napoleon's mistresses would be ushered in before him while he was still at his desk, and curtly told to go straight to the bed. He would then join the lucky, or unlucky woman for a matter of minutes.

The royal Palace of St Cloud,* right *on the River Seine in western Paris, was re-opened in 1802. Josephine found its huge marble staircases and ornate galleries too majestic. She missed the intimate mood of Malmaison

Madame Grassini* above, *the great prima donna of Milan, proved a match for the conquering lion of France. She won more attention than many of Napoleon's mistresses, but less than her pride demanded. She finally eloped with a musician of her own Bohemian temperament

Jean-Loup Charmet

With Mademoiselle Georges, a 16-year-old actress with the face and body of a Greek goddess, Napoleon enjoyed horseplay and practical jokes. But on one occasion when this good-humoured and high-spirited teenager was in bed with the First Consul he had an alarming respiratory attack. Thinking that he was dying in her company, 'Georgina' panicked, and the whole of the Tuileries was woken by the sound of her screams. Aides-de-camp and Josephine in her negligée rushed to Napoleon's bedside to find him perfectly recovered, and deeply embarrassed, while a scantily clad Mademoiselle George sobbed. It was not long before she disappeared from Napoleon's love-life, and she was not sorry.

Josephine's insecurity

At first Josephine was deeply upset and constantly tearful about her husband's affairs. She spent more time, at least an hour in the mornings, on her make-up and Napoleon made unkind jokes about the impact of her frequent tears on the powder and rouge. She even suggested that his occupancy of the marital bed was necessary for national security. Since she

Mansell Collection

was such a light sleeper, she argued, she would be sure to wake and alert the guards in the event of a night-time assassination attempt. She was now totally, abjectly in love with the man she had so diffidently married: 'I want always to remain in your eyes the good, the tender Josephine, solely concerned with your happiness.' Her ladies-in-waiting, even her children, advised her against making scenes when she was jealous because it was clear that Napoleon was not serious about his mistresses, a point he made repeatedly. He insisted that, with Britain rallying European forces against French domination, he was far too busy to fall in love, and his wife's insecurity only irritated him and made him love her less.

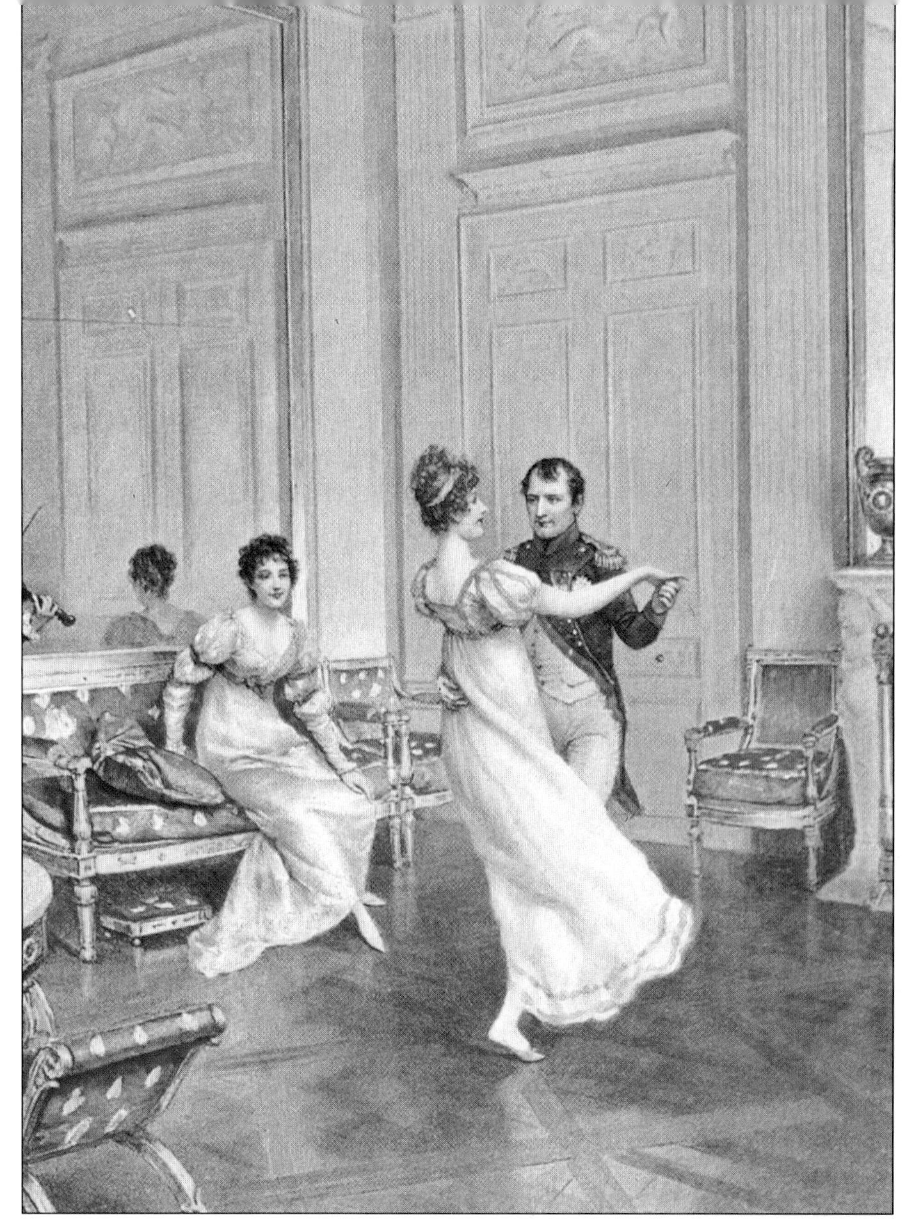

The Emperor above ***delighted in entertaining a succession of beautiful mistresses. A number of such liaisons had an Imperial theme: ambassadors from across Europe kept their ruling houses informed of Napoleon's tastes in women, his relations with Josephine, and the dances which he preferred. Another beauty was always on hand to replace a discarded favourite***

'I always wanted to remain in your eyes the good, the tender Josephine, solely concerned with your happiness.'

JOSEPHINE TO NAPOLEON

But the case of Adèle Duchâtel, identified only as 'Madame X' until this century, represented a more serious threat to the marriage, because she was an aristocratic, accomplished young lady who, as Josephine's reader, had been introduced to and became intimate with Napoleon. To the horror of her attendants, Josephine insisted on surprising her husband while he was alone with Adèle Duchâtel, and found them both in a 'disorderly state'. Instead

Delaroche: Napoleon in his Cabinet, Agnew & Sons, London/Bridgeman

♔ ***Napoleon's stout, self-dramatized appearance* above *was ridiculed by those who did not sense his magnetic power, as well as those who were jealous of it. One French general said he feared neither God nor the Devil, but could tremble like a child when he approached Napoleon. Of his greatness, the Emperor felt no doubt***

of being shamed, Napoleon went quite wild with anger, smashing china and bawling at his wife to leave him alone. But he was soon bored with Adèle Duchâtel, partly because she too obviously sought to capitalize on her position, and Josephine was only too happy to dismiss her. Madame Duchâtel was summoned before her and told that Napoleon had intimated that he would be 'very displeased by any display of affection which you might think yourself authorized to give him.'

However, Josephine's relief was always short-lived, for new liaisons followed in quick succession.

Gradually, and even then only fitfully, Josephine accepted Napoleon on his own terms: 'I must have distractions. I am a man apart and no one is going to tell me what to do.' She tried to control the situation by choosing the mistresses herself. She knew her husband's taste and so she would hire lady 'readers' who were inevitably invited to stay with the emperor after they had shut their books.

But others could play this game. Pauline Borghese's personal retinue consisted of sweet-faced blondes chosen for their likely appeal to her brother and the wily Caroline Murat knew what she was doing when she set up a former schoolmate of Hortense, Eléonore Denuelle, as the mistress who would prove the Emperor's fertility. Throughout the brief liaison, and her subsequent pregnancy, this young lady was strictly chaperoned, so that Napoleon would be in no doubt as to the paternity of the resulting child.

As Napoleon saw it, the question of remarriage was quite separate from the question of marital fidelity. He had contempt for his family's eagerness for a divorce and when the statesman Talleyrand asked for his views on the subject he said, 'How can I abandon her now, just because I have become greater than when she married me?' Because it had become a question of politics, he even discussed divorce with Josephine. Knowing well that the man who had 19 horses killed under him in battle had less courage in front of his tearful wife, she sweetly said that when or if he wished for a divorce she would oblige him with as much dignity as she could muster. He, however, would have to take the initiative so that the world would know that it was not her real will.

> ***'I must have distractions. I am a man apart and no one is going to tell me what to do.'***
>
> NAPOLEON TO JOSEPHINE

Napoleon's scruples about Josephine's happiness hid the convenience of her age – she was 40 in 1803 – as his excuse for not having a child. If he were to marry some young princess who then failed to get pregnant, he would look ridiculous. But on the last day of December 1806, while he was in Poland after his recent victory over the Prussian and Russian armies, he received a letter from Caroline Murat telling him that Eléonore Denuelle had borne him a son on 13 December. This birth was not conclusively reassuring, because Napoleon's own spies discovered that Eléonore had also been General Murat's lover. He would have to wait and see whether the baby looked like a Bonaparte. But in the meantime, the news gave him confidence and the list of eligible princesses was studied in earnest. Then, on the first day of 1807, he laid eyes on the only woman besides Josephine who captured his heart.

Marie de Walewska

Her name was Marie de Walewska and she was the 19-year-old wife of a 70-year-old Polish count. With snow glinting on her fair hair, she stood by the road to Warsaw to watch the French champion of Polish liberty as he passed. Napoleon's current enemies – Prussia, Austria and Russia – were the enemies of Polish independence and when Polish noblemen noticed his interest in the lovely young countess, they prevailed upon Marie to go to the ball in his honour. As a patriot she was urged to reciprocate the French emperor's love at first sight and Napoleon spoke seductively in such terms. 'Think how much dearer your country will be to me if you take pity on my poor heart.'

Marie claimed that patriotism overrode her moral scruples about becoming Napoleon's lover and that, 'at the moment of consummation of the sacrifice' she fainted right away. But, on St Helena, Napoleon remembered wryly that Marie had not struggled 'overmuch'. She cannot have been a complete innocent for she already had a baby by her husband, but Napoleon did intimidate her. It was significant that she recalled him in terms reminiscent of Josephine's. He was a strangely touching 'volcano' of a man; she was a mere dove to his eagle. For his part, Napoleon thought Marie's

attrib. to Robert Lefevre: Empress Josephine/E.T. Archive

♔ ***The deceptively languid Josephine*** above, ***although brought up simply on the tiny island of Martinique and largely uneducated, carried out the role of Empress with great dignity and style. Her natural, unaffected manners charmed not only foreign royalty by also the most menial court officials***

Regnault: Marriage of Prince Jerome Bonaparte and Princess of Würtemberg, Versailles/© Photo RMN

♔ ***The Emperor and Empress in full regal splendour*** left ***attend the wedding of Jerome Bonaparte and Princess Catherine of Württemberg at the Tuileries in 1807. But neither ever felt fully at ease with the increasing formality of Imperial court life. Napoleon could find distraction on the battlefield and frequently in the arms of other women. Josephine, however, yearned for the carefree gaiety of Malmaison days, as her husband increasingly distanced himself from her***

Gerard: Portrait of Marie Walewska, Versailles/© Photo RMN

Marie de Walewska* above *was in a different class to Napoleon's previous mistresses. Sweet-natured, virtuous and devoutly religious, she was dazzled by Napoleon's attentions. He, in turn, displayed great tenderness towards her, and admired particularly her burning love for Poland

soul was as lovely as her face, and the fact that this religious and gentle young woman was ambitious for her country rather than for herself aroused his finer feelings. Josephine was alarmed. When her husband started talking about a woman's soul, something was seriously amiss.

The beginning of the end

Josephine had been left by Napoleon and his army at Mainz in Germany. He had been distraught once entranced by Marie, he did everything to dissuade his wife from joining him for the coldest months of the winter, when the fighting ceased. The distance was too great, he told her, the roads too bad. He retreated to a fortified Prussian castle with Marie, sending Josephine back to Paris to preside over the imperial court and – this was an order – to be cheerful. When she hinted at the affair in her letters his harsh commands were mixed with a deceitful tenderness. 'I love only my little Josephine, sweet, pouting and capricious, who can quarrel with grace – as she does everything else, for she is always lovable except when she is jealous; and then she becomes a she-devil.'

The Empress, bored by the increasingly formal court, was made more miserable by the sudden death of four-year-old Napoleon-Charles after an attack of croup. Hortense, now Queen of Holland, was inconsolable, and the tragedy resulted in a short-lived reconciliation between she and her husband Louis, which produced a son, Louis-Napoleon, eventually Napoleon III.

'How can I abandon her now, just because I have become greater than when she married me.'

NAPOLEON TO JOSEPHINE

It was ten months after the poignant parting at Mainz before Napoleon rejoined Josephine in France on 27 July 1808. He was affectionate towards her, and she told her son that she had every reason to trust in his enduring love and his sense of justice. But others noticed a new distance in the Emperor's relations with his Empress, and a new separation in their daily lives. After Josephine received a letter from one of Napoleon's ministers asking her to initiate divorce proceedings in the interests

Mary Evans Picture Library

Josephine was summoned to the chateau at Fontainebleu in the autumn of 1809. But only after her arrival did she learn that Napoleon had had the door connecting their suites sealed by workmen. This picture conveys the depth of her shock

of France, she became agitated. When challenged, Napoleon professed to be angered by the crudity of the initiative, and condemned his minister's 'misplaced zeal'. He simply lacked the courage to be honest and reassured her out of guilt and remorse.

It was obvious to everyone but Josephine that he was bent on remarriage. It was decided that an alliance with either a Russian grand-duchess or an Austrian arch-duchess would be most useful. But an indiscretion of Josephine's, intentional or not, may have scotched the first, Russian possibility. A remark suggesting that her husband was often impotent reached the ears of the tsar's court.

A false alarm

Tormented by sorrow at the need to 'marry a womb', Napoleon could not come clean with his wife. In the spring of 1808 he told Talleyrand that he had reached the final decision, and that he would talk to Josephine. A play was scheduled for that evening's entertainment at the Tuileries and those courtiers in the know were tense with expectation. Then it was announced that the play would proceed without their imperial majesties because the Emperor was unwell. After the performance Talleyrand and Madame de Rémusat went to enquire after his health, only to be told that at eight o'clock he had bolted his doors and retired to bed with Josephine. 'What a devil of a man!' the infuriated Talleyrand exclaimed.

Soon after, Josephine accompanied Napoleon on an extended tour of south-west France and northern Spain. He was negotiating the fate of Spain, in the grip of civil war, with its exiled royal family; he solved the problem by putting his own brother Joseph on the throne. Though the château where they stayed for most of the time was shabby, and though travelling gave Josephine migraines, this trip represented the Indian summer of the imperial couple's love. Away from the stuffy court, they ran hand-in-

© Collection Viollet

After Napoleon declared his intention to divorce her, Josephine fainted. One of Napoleon's aides helped to revive her, and here looks up reproachfully at the Emperor who, fired by a sense of destiny, seems finally able to place his political need to remarry above his love for his wife

THE ART OF REVOLUTION

The paintings of Jacques-Louis David chronicle the upheavals of France before and during the Napoleonic era. When the Revolution broke out on the streets of Paris, David became intoxicated by the fast-changing events. He aligned himself with the new leader, Robespierre so closely that he was jailed after Robespierre's execution.

Soon, David was to fall under a new spell. After carrying out his coup d'etat, Napoleon was quick to realize that his plans could be promoted by David's magnificently theatrical compositions in oil. Some of the most famous images of Napoleon were to be created by David, such as the heroic 'Napoleon Crossing the Alps' *right*

David: Napoleon Crossing the Alps, Malmaison/Bridgeman/Giraudon

NAPOLEON'S EMPIRE

Napoleon reached his decision in 1809 to divorce Josephine at a time when his fortunes and power were reaching their zenith. As Emperor of France, he had under his control the Illyrian Provinces, a number of the Papal States, Tuscany, Holland and the German states bordering the Northern Sea. The territories of the Swiss Confederation, the Grand Duchy of Warsaw and the Confederation of the Rhine were all closely bound by various treaties to Napoleon's Empire.

Bonaparte leaned resourcefully on his large family to secure and hold a group of vassal states encircling the Empire. The print *below*, published at the time when Bonaparte was master of Europe, shows Napoleon and his brothers astride the globe. Joseph Bonaparte was given the demanding role of King of Spain; Jerome ruled the Kingdom of Westphalia and Josephine's son, Eugène, was appointed Viceroy of the Italian Kingdom. Joachim Murat, the husband of Napoleon's sister Caroline, ruled Naples and another brother-in-law, Felix Bacciochi, the husband of Elisa, ruled the Principality of Lucca and Piombino.

With his marriage to Marie-Louise in 1810, Napoleon ruled a vast Empire to which even Austria was now bound. The birth a year later of his heir, named as King of Rome, seemed to secure the dynasty. 'To take hold of the world,' the Emperor wrote, 'he will only have to stretch out his hands.'

The Emperor's 'family tree' *left* includes vignettes of both Josephine and Marie Louise. As an Imperial prince and princess, Eugène and Hortense are also depicted; indeed, the Imperial succession passed to Hortense's son, Napoleon III

Musée Carnavalet/Jean Loup Charmet

Musée Carnavalet/Jean Loup Charmet

hand along sandy beaches, and he teased and joked with her as in the old days.

When war, once more against the Austrians, reclaimed Napoleon's total concentration in the spring of 1809 he made secret preparations to leave for the Rhineland alone. It was not the Empress's inclination to move with him that bothered him so much as the tedium of arranging for the transport of her baggage and retinue. Before dawn, Josephine woke to hear the sound of a carriage departing. Without stockings on her slippered feet, she dashed down and clung to the carriage, pleading to be taken with him. Finding, as usual, that he could not bear the spectacle of Josephine in tears, Napoleon threw his own coat around her and ordered her baggage to be sent on later. They had reached Strasbourg before he insisted on leaving her. That was the last journey they made together.

It was the autumn of 1809, and Josephine

'She has embellished 13 years of my life. The memory of this will be forever engraved on my heart . . .'

NAPOLEON ON JOSEPHINE AT THEIR DIVORCE

was at Malmaison when she heard of Marie Walewska's pregnancy. After his defeat of the Prussians and Austrians, Napoleon had summoned the imperial physician rather than his wife to Vienna. He had to verify Marie's pregnancy and to prescribe how the countess, who had been installed in a little house near the palace of Schönbrunn, should live while she was expecting the French emperor's child. As a consolation, Josephine received 800 shrubs and bulbs from the Hapsburg nurseries for her hothouse – 'these are my children' she once said of her flowers. It was October before her husband ordered her to proceed to Fontainebleau, where he would join her within a matter of days: 'I am happy at the thought of seeing you and await the moment with impatience.' Nevertheless, the order to seal up the door linking his apartments with Josephine's was made before Napoleon returned. For her it was small comfort that Napoleon could not trust himself to be alone with her. Now she knew the end was truly nigh.

Schopin: Divorce of Napoleon & Josephine, Reproduced by permission of the Trustees of the Wallace Collection

The divorce papers were signed left ***in the throne room at the Palace of the Tuileries on the evening of 15 December 1809. Invitations were sent out as to a ball. Josephine endured the ordeal in front of many people who bore her a long-standing animosity. After she had formally signed the papers, Napoleon kissed her, took her hand, and led her with dignity to her chambers***

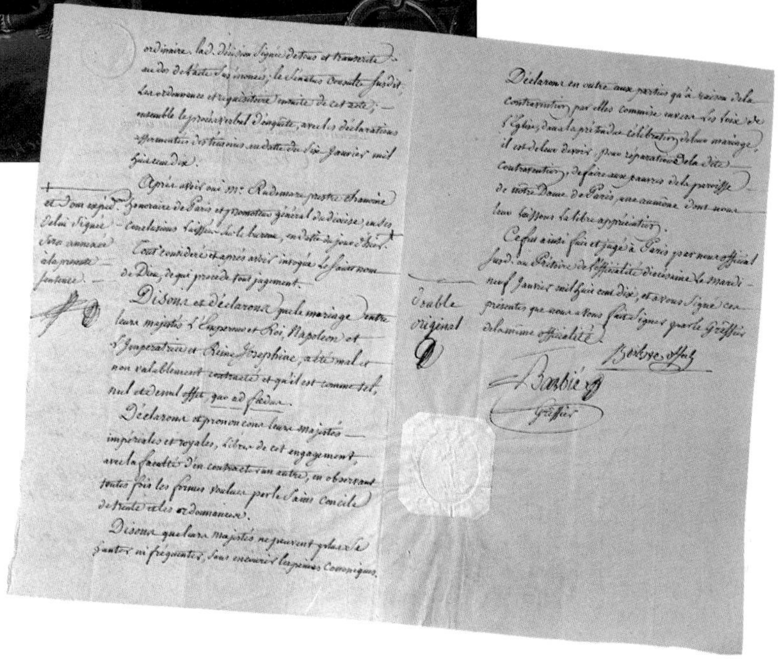

For five weeks after his return to France, Napoleon tried to get various intermediaries, including Hortense and Eugène, to tell Josephine of his decision, but they refused. On the night of 30 November 1809 the imperial couple dined together. Josephine was silent and tense, while Napoleon trembled with nervousness and constantly gazed upon her with a look of acute anguish. Alone together in the drawing room he broke the news to her. Within minutes a senior palace official was summoned, and he saw that Josephine was lying full-length on the floor and moaning pitifully. He helped Napoleon to carry her to her apartments, where her ladies and in due course Hortense set about reviving and calming her.

Divorce

It took just over two weeks to make the divorce settlement, which was formalized before a council of senate officials and family members. For this grim occasion Josephine recovered her gracious composure and wore a simple white dress. Although pale and strained, she braved the barely disguised satisfaction of her in-laws – Pauline Borghese had held parties to celebrate the divorce – and heard her moist-eyed husband declare, 'I can on the contrary (to any complaint about his wife's character) only congratulate myself on the affection and tenderness of my well-beloved wife. She has embellished 13 years of my life; the memory of this will be for ever engraved on my heart. She has been crowned by my hand; it is my desire that she should retain the rank and title of Crowned Empress, but above all that she should never doubt my affection and that she should always regard me as her best and dearest friend.'

Jean-Loup Charmet

The deeds of separation above ***were drawn up in two weeks. Josephine was given an allowance of some three million francs a year and her debts of two million francs were cleared. She was allowed the estates of Malmaison and the Elysée Palace and permitted to retain the title of 'Majesty'***

Josephine responded with a speech which had been approved by Napoleon. 'I have to declare that having no longer any hope of bearing children who could fulfil the needs of his policies and the interest of France, I am pleased to offer him the greatest proof of attachment and devotion that has ever been given on this earth . . .' At this point she broke down, and the rest of her text was read aloud by the Secretary of State.

On the following day, in driving rain, a heavily veiled Josephine left the Tuileries for Malmaison, where she was soon joined by Hortense and Eugène. In the same rain, downcast Napoleon set off for Trianon in the company of his mother and sisters. Next day he visited Josephine at Malmaison. As soon as his carriage was visible, she went to the courtyard to meet him. He gave her his arm and they strolled together through the wet gardens. But the servants noticed that they had not embraced and that he was careful to remain within sight of the château windows.

RELICS OF EMPIRE

The combination of Josephine's spendthrift nature and the enormous wealth and plunder accumulated by Napoleon in his military and political careers meant that the Bonapartes acquired a vast collection of treasures from all over Europe. Perhaps their most treasured possessions, however, were those with a more personal touch, recalling the rare and precious times they spent together as a family

Before the advent of photography, those who could afford them carried miniature portraits of their loved ones. The miniature below ***of Napoleon in military dress was made by court painter Jean Baptiste Isabey***

Brumaire

This sumptuous parure, or set of jewels left, ***originally belonged to Marie Antoinette. They disappeared from view for a while after the Revolution, and when they re-emerged, Napoleon bought them for Josephine. The tiara, necklace, brooch, rings and earrings contain sapphires in a setting of diamonds, Josephine bequeathed them to Hortense, who sold them later on to the Duke of Orléans, who, as Louis-Philippe ruled from 1830 to 1848 as the last king of France***

Jean-Loup Charmet

Napoleon was particularly fond of Josephine's children, and treasured a writing set above ***which was a gift from Hortense. It is covered in gilded Napoleonic motifs – eagles, bees and a crowned N – and contains a pencase and penknife cased in gilt and enamel. Between the inkwells is mounted a miniature, probably by Isabey, of Hortense and her children***

To mark his accession in 1804 the people of Paris presented the new Emperor with a silver-gilt table service in the classical style which came, under the patronage of Napoleon, to be known as Empire. One of the most impresive pieces was the boat-shaped nef left, ***a receptacle for table-napkins, cruets and cutlery***

END OF THE EMPIRE

THE COLLAPSE OF NAPOLEON AND JOSEPHINE'S RELATIONSHIP MIRRORED THE CRUMBLING OF THEIR EMPIRE. AS JOSEPHINE'S STAR WANED AFTER THE DIVORCE, SO TOO NAPOLEON'S MILITARY PROWESS WAS DIMINISHED BY SUCCESSIVE DEFEATS

After her divorce, Josephine stayed on for a while at Malmaison below *before the arrival of Marie-Louise in Paris forced her to retreat to Normandy. She never reconciled herself to life at Navarre, and returned to Malmaison, where she and Napoleon had enjoyed the happiest years of their marriage, whenever she could*

BEFORE THE DIVORCE HAD BEEN FINALIZED Napoleon had asked for the hand in marriage of Arch Duchess Marie-Louise of Austria. There is even evidence that Josephine facilitated this bid by telling the wife of Metternich, the Austrian foreign minister, how much she welcomed the match. She said she could only justify the sacrifice she had made if it paid off in real terms – that is, if the new Empress represented an important political alliance and gave birth to the child Napoleon and France wanted so much. Certainly, her honourable and devoted son seems to have felt no embarrassment at his role in the proceedings. Eugène de Beauharnais was broker for the proxy marriage between the Austrian Emperor's daughter and Napoleon, which took place in Vienna in March 1810.

Josephine without Napoleon

Josephine's tears continued for months after the divorce, but they trickled down a miraculously uncontorted face. The Emperor's ex-wife was capable of weeping with a certain style and until Marie-Louise of Austria actually arrived in France she enjoyed a false calm.

Josephine had no rival yet and she had the consolation of knowing that Napoleon was equally sad and still in close touch. He drove to see her at Malmaison and said that these visits reminded him of 'what charms your company has for me'. In his regular letters he urged her, for his sake, to be happy and to trust in his undying affection rather than the malicious rumours that always circulated around Paris.

The humiliating and practical implications of the divorce became obvious when Marie-Louise arrived on French soil at the end of March. Apart from the fact that Napoleon was obviously preoccupied with his 'womb', Josephine had to endure the defection of many members of her household to the new court. Napoleon insisted that she retain the prestige and life-style of an Empress, even against her personal inclination, but only the most doggedly loyal of her ladies-in-waiting and attendants volunteered to remain with what was in effect a second-class imperial household. Even her famous hairdresser, who owed his reputation to her patronage, deserted to Marie-Louise. Moreover, Napoleon's 19-year-old bride had no generous feelings towards her predecessor, so that Josephine's hope of becoming a fond

Garnier: Entry of Napoleon & Marie Louise to the Tuileries on their wedding day, Versailles/Bridgeman/Giraudon

dowager figure was soon dashed.

Despite his high-minded utterances on Josephine's status, Napoleon was at first less than gallant to her. When the proxy marriage took place he bestowed upon his ex-wife, in addition to the generous divorce settlement, the château and duchy of Navarre in Normandy. But this gift came with a sting, for it was made clear that Josephine would be advised to live there. At her beloved Malmaison she was too near the jealous and haughty new Empress for comfort. This was a bitter blow to Josephine, who was always happiest near Paris and fashionable metropolitan life, and who found that her vast château in Normandy was almost derelict.

'what charms your company has for me'

NAPOLEON TO JOSEPHINE

At least, the new Duchess of Navarre thought, not for the first time, she had the unstinting love of her children and grandchildren. She spent a happy summer with Hortense, whose husband had recently abdicated as King of Holland, at Aix-les-Bains, where she was visited twice by the ever-faithful Eugène.

However, Josephine was unsure of her future and in desperation had written an extremely formal letter to Napoleon, asking him to tell her plainly where she could settle in peace and dignity. In his pointedly intimate reply, he chided her for thinking he had changed.

Through, Eugène, Napoleon made adequate funds available for the renovation of the house and grounds at Navarre. While this work was being done, Josephine travelled around

Napoleon consummated his union with Marie-Louise a week before their state wedding **above.** ***He described his young bride as 'good, sweet, naive and fresh as roses'***

The birth of the King of Rome in 1811 fulfilled Napoleon's dynastic hopes. He lavished great care and love on the boy **below,** ***who died of tuberculosis in exile in 1832***

Meissonier: Napoleon on Campaign, Musée d'Orsay, Paris/Bridgeman/Giraudon

♔ *Though Napoleon continued to lead his armies from the front* above, *the campaigns he undertook in his later years lacked some of his earlier verve*

♔ *With France invaded on two fronts, and Paris in his enemies' hands, Napoleon signed an Act of Abdication* below *at Fontainebleau on 13 April 1814*

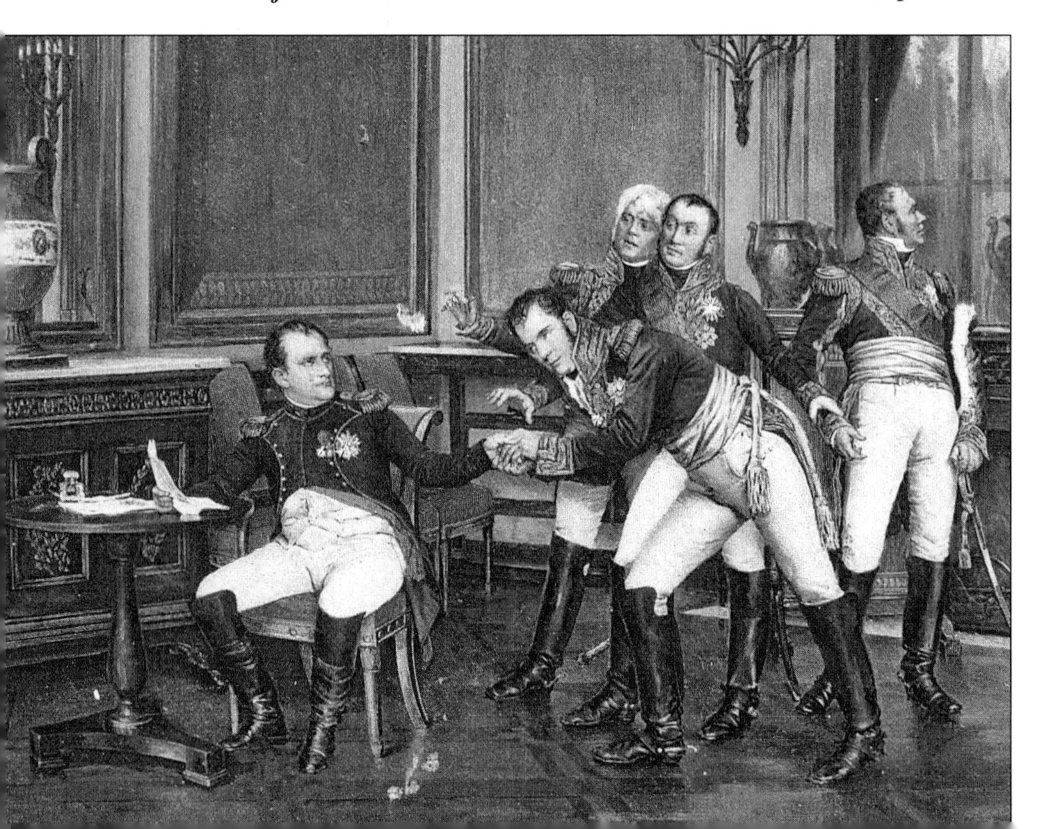

Switzerland, and there she heard of Marie-Louise's pregnancy. To the best wishes she sent to Paris, Napoleon replied, 'Yes, the Empress is in her fourth month of pregnancy. She is feeling very well and is very fond of me.'

The King of Rome

When, in March 1811, church bells announced the birth of Napoleon's baby son, who was titled the King of Rome, Josephine was prompt with her congratulations and she organized a celebratory ball at Navarre. Within days Napoleon had despatched Eugène to Normandy with a personal thank-you note. His son was big and sturdy. 'He has my chest, my mouth and my eyes. I hope he will fulfil his destiny.' Now that Marie-Louise's mission had been accomplished, Josephine's position eased and she was permitted to spend the spring months at Malmaison.

Josephine regained her serenity, lost her migraines and, for the first time in her life, put on weight. Napoleon joked that she would soon resemble a Normandy farmer's wife. She even invited Marie de Walewska to Malmaison, in order to see Napoleon's illegitimate son.

Just before he left for his disastrous inva-

Viger: Empress Josephine presenting her children to Emperor Alexander, Private Collection/Bridgeman Art Library

The conquering Tsar Alexander showed great gallantry towards Josephine on her return to Malmaison in April 1814. He was introduced to her children and grandchildren left ***and dined with her several times before her death a few weeks later***

In her later life, as Duchess de Navarre, Josephine lost her slender, graceful figure. Napoleon teased her by writing, 'I hear that you are as plump as a good Normandy farm wife.' The miniature above ***by Jean-Baptiste Isabey was painted in 1813***

Isabey: Josephine, Duchess of Navarre, Cabinet des Arts Graphique, Louvre © Photo RMN

sion of Russia, in the summer of 1812, Napoleon obliged Josephine by arranging for her to see his legitimate son. Without the knowledge of Marie-Louise and with the connivance of the governess, Josephine spent an hour with the little King of Rome in a house in the Bois de Boulogne. The nursemaid commented afterwards, 'Goodness, this one's nice. She's said more to me in a quarter of an hour than the other one has in six months.' No one knows if Napoleon was present. If he was it was the last meeting between him and Josephine.

Napoleon without Josephine

When Josephine had arrived at the Navarre château for the first time Marie-Louise had made her triumphal entry into Paris. The bridal party had been met at the forest of Compiègne. Although Marie-Louise had grown up fearing Napoleon as the enemy of Austria and a veritable ogre, she seems to have been pleasantly surprised by the husband who leapt into her carriage. She allowed Napoleon to consummate the marriage that very night, rather than after the blessing ceremony in Paris, and on the morning after he pronounced, 'Marry a German girl; they make the best wives in the world – good, sweet, naive and fresh as roses.' At least the plump and giggling Marie-Louise had been bred for the stuffy rituals of court life and she did not expect to marry for love.

In his concern for Josephine's welfare Napoleon was aware of the popularity of 'la vieille' (the old one) with the French people generally and his soldiers in particular. For them, his first wife was 'Our Lady of Victory' who had brought him luck. By August 1813, it seemed that there was something to this belief, because in that month Napoleon's illustrious Austrian father-in-law joined the allies against him, and October saw his first great defeat at Leipzig. Then, while the Continental allies pushed into northern France, the British invaded from Spain. By March 1814 Paris was occupied and in April Napoleon abdicated and was exiled to the island of Elba.

Josephine and her children were more loyal to Napoleon than his own family. His last letter to her, written in the month of his abdication, has the bitterness of a betrayed man. Bernadotte, the Crown Prince of Sweden who had married his first love, Desirée Clary, turned against him; Caroline and General Murat deserted him to hang onto their tottering throne at Naples; brothers Jerome and Joseph bungled their responsibilities; General Marmont had handed Paris over; Talleyrand had deceived everyone. The list of the ungrateful was long.

Adieu, my dear Josephine

'They have betrayed me; yes, all of them except our dear Eugène, so worthy of you and me ... Adieu, my dear Josephine. Resign yourself as I am doing and never forget one who will never forget you.' With a certain poignancy he added that his health was not good and that he hoped to hear from her in Elba. Josephine would have been glad to join him in exile, but she held back while there was even a faint chance, that Marie-Louise would be persuaded to go.

In the meantime, Josephine set about ensuring the safe future of Hortense and Eugène by entertaining the Russian Tsar Alexander. Young and romantic, the Russian ruler was enchanted by the style and charm of the 50-year-old first Empress. He became a regular at Malmaison, where flowers bloomed and swans still glided on the lake, and where the cuisine was legendary. He was expected for dinner on the day in May 1814 when Josephine had to take to her gilded bed after a chilling carriage ride, and he sent his own doctor to attend her when the symptoms worsened. Just over a week later, on 29 May 1814, she died of diphtheria.

When the news reached Elba, Napoleon was 'grievously smitten' and for several days he shut himself away in his rooms, refusing to see anyone but his grand marshal. Almost a year later, during the 'Hundred Days' back in France, he found time to hear the details of Josephine's death at first hand, from Hortense and from the doctor, and to visit Malmaison. Wandering about the place that so evoked Josephine's spirit, he could not believe that she was dead, and half-expected, half-hoped that he would come across her gathering flowers in the garden. After his defeat at Waterloo, and before his second exile, he returned to Malmaison to spend some of his last days on French soil with Josephine's ghost. A portrait of her adorned the wall of Napoleon's bedroom on the rocky island of St Helena, and it was in his line of vision when he died in 1821. His last word was 'Josephine!'

'The most enchanting being I have ever known.'

NAPOLEON ON JOSEPHINE DURING HIS LAST VISIT TO MALMAISON

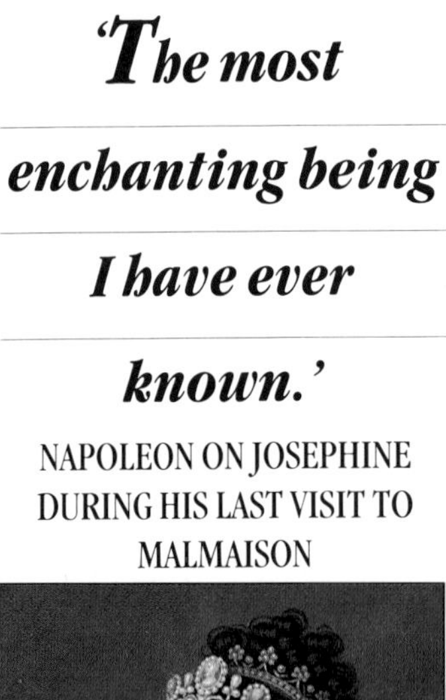

Quaglia: Josephine in 1814, Reproduced by permission of the Trustees of the Wallace Collection

EXILE ON ST HELENA

Steuben: Napoleon at St. Helene, Ile d'Aix Musée Napoleonien/© Photo RMN-G. Blot

Following his defeat at Waterloo in 1815, the British sent Napoleon into his final exile on the remote southern Atlantic island of Saint Helena. He arrived on 15 October 1815 with an entourage of several loyal companions. They stayed at Longwood, a house which was originally built for the lieutenant governor.

Napoleon's life settled down into a regular routine. He slept late, breakfasting about 10 a.m. Although he was allowed to go anywhere on the island provided that a British officer accompanied him, he confined himself to the Longwood grounds. He passed the day writing and talking, and dined at 7 p.m. He generally spent the evening reading, writing and playing cards.

Although he kept his mind active, Napoleon was like a caged animal on the small island. Life was monotonous without the support of a close companion. Josephine *above, left*, in 1814 was dead, and Marie-Louise had become the mistress of Count von Neipperg, the Austrian officer who had been appointed to watch over her. She sent no letters or news of their son.

At the end of 1817, Napoleon fell ill with an ulcer or a cancer of the stomach. His condition rapidly worsened at the beginning of 1821. From March of that year he was confined to his bed. In April he dictated his last testament, asking that his ashes be laid to rest on the banks of the Seine. He died on May 5. Against his last wishes, he was buried in the Rupert Valley on St Helena, his grave marked by a stone saying 'Ci-Git' – 'Here Lies'.